7-3-71

Elysion

ELYSION

ON ANCIENT GREEK AND ROMAN
BELIEFS CONCERNING
A LIFE AFTER DEATH

by W. F. JACKSON KNIGHT

with an introduction by
G. WILSON KNIGHT

And what the dead had no speech for, when living,
They can tell you, being dead: the communication
Of the dead is tongued with fire beyond the language of the living.
T. S. ELIOT, *Little Gidding*

RIDER & COMPANY · LONDON

RIDER & COMPANY
178–202 Great Portland Street, London W1

AN IMPRINT OF THE HUTCHINSON GROUP

London Melbourne Sydney
Auckland Johannesburg Cape Town
and agencies throughout the world

First published 1970

*This book has been set in Bembo type, printed in Great Britain
on antique wove paper by Anchor Press, and
bound by Wm. Brendon, both of Tiptree, Essex*

ISBN 0 09 104150 3 (cased)
0 09 104151 1 (paper)

CONTENTS

For Olivia Mordue

Introduction

During the last years of his life Jackson Knight was engaged in planning, and reading for, a comprehensive investigation, to be entitled *Elysion*, into the death-beliefs of ancient Greece and Rome. But this was only one among his many commitments. He had more on his hands than he could master; and when he died in 1964 the book had not been completed.

Elysion was inspired equally by my brother's life-long devotion to the Classics and by his experiences of modern Spiritualism. Of these experiences and his published records of them my account must be postponed until the completion of a volume by various hands of Essays on his life and work. In my present Introduction I shall refer to four relevant articles only. These are: 'My Conviction of the Truth', *Two Worlds* 65, 3394/5 (13/20 December 1952), posthumously reissued in *Light* 85, 3461 (Summer 1965); 'The After-Life in Greek and Roman Antiquity', *Folklore* 69 (December 1958); 'Spiritualism among the Ancients', a lecture delivered to the College of Psychic Science on 27 November 1962 and published posthumously in *Light* 85, 3462 (Autumn 1965); and 'Origins of Belief', *Folklore* 74 (Spring 1963).

His earliest plan-sheet for the main study suggested a weighty book of packed learning, and it was this, or one of similar quality, that was in his mind. But both his friend and secretarial supporter Miss Olivia Mordue and myself were always urging him to complete a version of slighter proportions. My own conviction was that it should not be over-weighted with learning, but rather a flowing and lucid account readable and informative alike for scholar, student, and non-specialist.

About the time of his 1958 *Folklore* article he roughed out some fifty pages of manuscript covering the whole story in outline, but in 1963 we were still waiting for the more comprehensive account. In response to our anxieties, he in that year, or perhaps early in 1964, composed, independently of the first, a longer version of 135 pages which he left, in case of accidents, to meet our pleadings. It had been written under pressure, poured out from a full mind without any checking of detail and with few references to sources. Some of the material was illogically ordered, as though a forgotten theme had been wedged in during composition as an afterthought. This version was not regarded by the author as final, and was to have been expanded to about twice its length (letter to John D. Christie, 17 September 1964).

Since each of the two versions contained material not in the other it was necessary to collate them, grafting phrases or sentences from the one into paragraphs of the other. It was, strangely, possible to use nearly all of both texts, since each was improved by amplification. The ordering was in places adjusted and the narrative divided into sections with caption headings. Certain passages were incorporated, either as additional pieces or as better versions of the same material in the main account, from the essays published in *Folklore* in 1958 and *Light* in 1965 (p. 7 above).★

So much was within the sphere of my own editorial capacities. But this was only the beginning. My brother's writing had

★ It may be helpful to note these, as follows. From *Folklore* (December 1958): on p. 55 below, 'Often the deity . . . Homer's poetry.'; 'A god to us . . . as angels.'; 'it is surely fair . . . Olympian Family.'; on p. 96, 'Colonel H. R. Dixon-Smith . . . don't believe it.'; on p. 161, 'We must . . . Greek antiquity.'; on p. 163, Myers' verse-translation of Porphyry's lines; and on p. 177, 'a spirit-world exists . . . required.' From *Light* (Autumn 1965): on p. 88, the lines on Socrates from Aristophanes' *The Birds*. Also, from the unpublished 'Roman Ideas about Death' (see p. 111, note) the passage on p. 110, 'The *manes* were at first . . . ancestors'.

been hurried, unchecked, and submitted to no eye but my own. Before publication he would have checked details, added references, and submitted his text to a classical friend, or friends. This was now my business. The support given me by classical scholars has been generous (p. 18 below).

The final responsibility remains mine, and this responsibility goes farther than has yet been suggested. The nature of our hastily composed text, done in response to pressures, and the last and longer version when the author's health was failing, justifies a certain freedom, and I have accordingly exercised my own judgement so far as to include a few expansions and additions over and beyond the transpositions and collations already noted. These are listed below (p. 20).

None of the adjustments made have altered the work as my brother conceived it and meant it to appear. In the circumstances of its composition slips were inevitable and the corrections, smoothings, and amplifications are such as he would have approved. The editorial responsibility has been the less anxious in that *Elysion* does not aim to reverse past findings; there are no hazardous theories to be defended; it can say, with Shakespeare's Mark Antony, 'I tell you that which you yourselves do know'. Nevertheless it appears to me to be vividly, and in a new way, important.

The power derives from the author's acceptance, in general and with the obvious reservations understood, of the truths covered by what is today, though it is an age-old practice and belief, called 'Spiritualism'. This acceptance was stated firmly in his 1952 article 'My Conviction of the Truth' (p. 7 above). His direct experiences in this field date from 1950, but that he should have been ready for them is not strange. Some early lines of his, of about 1922, recently glanced at in the preface to my own *Gold-Dust: with other poetry* (1968; xxvi), were on spirit-powers in nature and beyond. I hope to discuss them in the biographical volume to which I have already referred.

Later, at Bloxham, he was from 1929 to 1935 actively engaged in the excavation of an ancient burial site, the results of which, noting the position of bones etc., he published in various journals and summed up in 'A Romano-British Site at Bloxham, Oxon.' in *Oxoniensia* III (1938). Soon after that, in *Cumaean Gates* (1936; reissued in *Vergil: Epic and Anthropology*, London 1967), he was researching into ancient mortuary ritual and belief and symbols of the soul's progress beyond death. There, and also in his 1938-9 work on Homer (published posthumously as *Many-Minded Homer*, London 1968), he was concerned to emphasise the reliance of Western culture on inspiratory sources from the East. These influences are felt strongly throughout *Elysion*, especially in discussion of the Pre-Socratic philosophers and the Neoplatonists. The doctrines of modern Spiritualism as delivered by spirit-entities have much in common with the ancient philosophies of India. He was always deeply concerned, as in his 1946 booklet *Poetic Inspiration*, with the twilit hinterlands of literary creation.

The core of his scholarly and poetic investigations had been from the start a trust planted in the mysteries. It is for this reason that he was an unusual scholar. We could say either that his work was more than 'scholarship', or that it was, in this field at least, the only real kind of scholarship, scholarship fully conscious of *that* for which such scholarship exists.

For would it not be strange, and most unsatisfactory, if all the researches into folklore and primitive ritual, such monumental labours as those of Frazer's *The Golden Bough*, were no more than exercises in inquisitiveness? Are they not impelled by a semi-awareness that somehow, embedded in the primitive mind as it rose from nature, are truths which the sophisticated intellect alone cannot reveal?* Too often the average scholar actually wishes to see himself as what Dr. Johnson, defining a lexicographer, called 'a harmless drudge'. He does himself a grave injustice. His achievements, like the lexicographer's, are indispensable; but they are only of use in preparation for the day when someone comes to show what it all means. The danger is

---

* The point is made by F. W. H. Myers, *Essays-Classical* (London 1883 etc.) 6.

that the strongholds of established scholarship, so justly proud of their professional skills, may claim for them a *final* superiority, and even begin to despise those mysteries which they exist to serve. The danger is apparent whenever the scholar, by the tone of a phrase or some subtle omission, tends to cloud, or blunt, some mystical or spiritualistic truth or fact, with suggestions of its absurdity. This is culture become suicidal.

It may seem that such polemics are uncalled for in introducing a work which, as I have said, makes no claims to discovery. But that is the whole point. The material is already well known, at least to specialists; and yet it has not been *seen*. Spiritualism is as old as man. Folklore and mythology, and probably religion too, are born of it; great literature, from the ancients down to our most acclaimed modern practitioners in drama and poetry, is saturated in it.* All these our universities study; and yet blindness on the main, the central, issue persists.

Even works of highest authority and value, while presenting and interpreting the relevant facts, somehow fail to awake a full perception. In the articles already noticed, 'My Conviction of the Truth' and 'The After-Life in Greek and Roman Antiquity', my brother pays tribute to F. W. H. Myers, Gilbert Murray, and Professor E. R. Dodds for their explorations into the psychic beliefs of the Ancients. His debts are most readily acknowledged. Of Erwin Rohde on the Pre-Socratic philosophers, he wrote:

Rohde, whose great chapters on these subjects must remain famous for a long time yet, cannot doubt the unifying principle; prophecy, purification and healing are all concerned with the world of spirits, and they are accessible to an ecstatic seer.

(*Folklore* 69, December 1958, 230)

---

* See my essay 'T. S. Eliot: some literary impressions' in *T. S. Eliot; the Man and his Work*, ed. Allen Tate (London 1967); and 'Masefield and Spiritualism', in *Mansions of the Spirit*, ed. G. A. Panichas (New York 1967). Both essays are included in my forthcoming volume *Neglected Powers* (London 1970).

Rohde's *Psyche*, now available in paperback, is a standard work of creative insight. But even here, despite my brother's tribute—and my remarks in this Introduction must not be attributed, directly or indirectly, to him— I would myself suggest that the weight of learning exposed, and the manifold and subtle distinctions made, inevitably set up barriers to an immediate and urgent response. They advance knowledge; but all knowledge is a kind of memorising, and quickly lapses; it is not necessarily experience. What is needed is that, while we are reading, we should see, and experience; for in these matters knowledge without experience dissolves.

I have referred to our most eminent academic authorities. I turn now to the other extreme: Mrs. St. Clair Stobart's *The Either-Or of Spiritualism* (London 1928). The title is sadly misleading, since it is not primarily a book on Spiritualism as such but one on Spiritualism among the Ancients; as found in Homer, Thales, Pherecydes, Empedocles, Iamblichus, St. Augustine, and others; and at the Delphic Oracle and the Eleusinian Mysteries. It draws on the relevant sources, though without numerical references. A bibliography of secondary sources is appended, prefaced by the legitimate claim that the material has been for the most part taken direct from the ancient authors themselves.

For such a book, aimed at a wide public, the absence of precise references may be in order. Mrs. Stobart is writing as a Spiritualist and in the cause of Spiritualism. Reading 'spiritualism' in a wide and general sense, her purpose is to show that classical culture was spiritualistically inspired. Homer's 'gods' are spirit-entities, and at the very heart of Greek culture was the Delphic Oracle as a centre of spiritualistic communion. So much granted, everything falls into place, and little more argument is required. Quotations from the various authors do all that is needed.

The trouble is that what Mrs. Stobart says is not only true, but obvious; and it is of central significance. And yet her book is unlikely to affect at all directly our seats of learning. The only aim of writing such a book, or indeed any book at all, is to

remove barriers to understanding; and to do that, especially
in this field, the barriers must be, at least provisionally, respected.
Identities which scholars only tentatively, and after great labour,
establish, and my brother in the following pages advances with
the most careful reservations, are by her quite rightly—for all
that she does is as inevitable and right from her viewpoint as
what Rohde and Dodds do from theirs—regarded as self-evident.

I have pointed to two main types of approach. Both are
at the same task, being concerned to indicate in what ways and
how far the ancients were involved in psychic practices and
beliefs. Both have their limitations, not so much in themselves
as in their effect. The one clouds us with a perfectly legitimate,
and for the purpose necessary, learning, so that we see less than
we know. With the other, truths so obvious are revealed that,
like large letters on a map, they are seen, but not read; and in this
case we know less than we see. What we need is the living experience of knowledge and sight combined, leading to recognition, or insight. This, for some strange reason, will not mature
from learning alone: the facts, as I have already stated, dissolve.

It will be clear why I think my brother's *Elysion* so important.
It is composed by one who was, like Myers, though with ad-
vantages in the progress of research and acceptance which
Myers scarcely enjoyed, both classical scholar and spiritualist.
He is at every point aware of both the claims of current scholarship and the truths of modern Spiritualism. This fusion in turn
makes possible its excellence of selection, keeping unswervingly
to the main theme with a background of unstressed scholarship
that knows what may be safely, for the immediate purpose,
disregarded. Hence, too, its urgency of appeal, fuelled, as
such urgency only could be, by the author's own experience
and belief. The text accordingly bears on it the impress of its
own conviction and therefore its own importance. Only in
this way, blending scholarship with belief, could so much of
the relevant material be so powerfully and lucidly delivered.
The great story is simply told, and the experience it induces is
compelling.

In linking modern Spiritualism to the Classics it performs a vital and challenging function. Today Spiritualism is steadily, on all its fronts, advancing; its public widens; but the fortresses of Church and University are still strong, and sometimes appear impregnable. Meanwhile our culture wilts; not only in the West, but in the East too, which is rapidly submitting to the encroachments of Western science and the parching of religious belief. Yet there are reservoirs waiting; the sluice-gates once opened, the waters will pour through, and in. This book is such a gate: a 'Cumaean Gate'.

For it not only states but forces recognition that those ancients whose wisdom and culture form, with Christianity, the traditional basis of our civilisation, were spiritualistically aware and spiritualistically impelled. Opening her chapter on the Delphic Oracle, Mrs. St. Clair Stobart writes:

At the time when the ancient Greek civilisation was at its apogee, when there were living in the same age a greater number of giant intellectuals than can be recalled for any other period in history, the Delphic Oracle was the officially recognised medium of communication between the inhabitants of two worlds. It was consulted by states, governments, philosophers, and emperors, and so far from being an object of ridicule, it was venerated and respected as an institution specially devised by the gods, or spirits, for the instruction and the counsel of mankind.

The statement is not excessive: it says less than what we are told in the *Oxford Classical Dictionary*.

With what might be called a truly shocking presumption our culture tries to ape the accomplishments of the past without recognition of those sources from which alone true virtue— 'virtue' in the old sense of virility and rectitude in one—derives.

Our book *Elysion* shows, moreover—and this could not be shown so effectively in a weightier book, the very speed of our reading being constituent to the recognition—how Christianity itself is less of a supernatural avatar than a cosmic flowering. As the Spirit of Apollonius tells us (p. 156 below), Christ came not to destroy, but to expand, the experience and wisdom of past ages. This is generally admitted so far as the Old Testament is concerned; but *Elysion* shows that it is equally true of the Greeks. 'Christ' is a Greek word, so is 'Logos'; the New Testament was written down in Greek. Christ and Paul lived within an area already saturated by Greek culture; and Christianity descends as much from the Greek as from the Hebrew. It is born from the marriage of the one with the other. That too is sometimes admitted; but it is not generally admitted that in their best wisdom the ancient Greeks and their descendants, from Hesiod to the Neoplatonists, were Spiritualists.*

Christianity might be called a 'super-spiritualism'. To understand its power through the ages we do well to see Christ as an archetype of man; that is, of all men. His mysterious birth from on high reflects our own, as described in Wordsworth's famous ode *On Intimations of Immortality*; his tragic suffering and death reflect ours; and his bodily resurrection reflects an assurance that our future existence is to be no less real and warm than that which we enjoy on earth. This much is reasonably clear; if it were not so, the appeal could not have been so poignant and enduring. But we can go farther. Just as the spiritualist, from ancient Egypt to our own time, has communion with relatives who have 'died', enjoys their companionship and enlists their help, so we are told by Christianity that Christ still lives and by power of the Spirit draws near to us, in support. He is, spiritualistically, the 'super-relative' of us all; and it is in this sense that Christianity, with the Church as 'medium', is a 'super-spiritualism'.

It may be forcefully argued that Christ and the Church are necessary; that reliance on our own 'dead', people like ourselves and perhaps not far advanced in the next sphere, is not

* The reliance of the New Testament on Egyptian mythology and ritual may be equally, or more, important: see Gerald Massey's essay, *The Historical Jesus and the Mythical Christ: what Christianity owes to Ancient Egypt*; privately printed 1887-8; republished for The Secular Society by The Pioneer Press (London 1921). The essay condenses material from Massey's major volumes, especially *The Natural Genesis* (London 1883), Vol. II, 378-503.

enough; and that we must hold before us, and draw strength and guidance from, the one central figure, the Christ, whose excellence is unquestioned. The Spiritualist would however say that he does not rely, in matters of high teaching, on his relatives, but on the many greater Guides whose wisdom is transmitted through mediums, and whose noble doctrines have in our own time already filled many books. But again, as is made clear in the following pages, the quality of the Guides we contact depends in part on our own spiritual state; and if, as the centuries revolve, the state of man sinks, and there is some evidence that it *is* sinking, shall we continue to make contact with the best? Are we, as modern Spiritualists, even when we think ourselves most independent, really still relying on the Christian tradition? Without it, would our spiritualism remain firm? Would the greater Guides still come to us?

The arguments, on both sides, are strong. But it is certain that, if Spiritualism without Christianity might become dangerous, the Church without Spiritualism is already withering; as may be seen in the many rearguard actions in which it so regularly and so unprofitably engages.* The desired end must surely be, as it is in my brother's book, a true blend, without mutual hostility, and with much give-and-take, of the Christian Church and Spiritualism. Such a consummation is, as Hamlet has it, 'devoutly to be wished'; and it is already adumbrated in England by the Churches' Fellowship for Psychical and Spiritual Studies, of which my brother was an active member, and Chairman of the Exeter Branch.

My brother's obligations in this book would have been recorded, in full, in his preface. First, he would have named Professor T. J. Haarhoff, who did so much to introduce him to

* The point is made by Canon J. D. Pearce-Higgins, Vice-Provost of Southwark, in a remarkable statement, sent in, at the suggestion of the Editor of *Psychic News*, to *The British Weekly* (15, 22 and 29 Feb. 1968) as an answer to attacks on Spiritualism in that journal. Extracts have been published in *Psychic News* (17 Feb. 1968). I would urge anyone who has doubts as to the Christian Church's failure to remain true to the spiritualistic elements of its basis to read Canon Pearce-Higgins' article.

spiritualistic experience, and the late Mrs. Margaret Lloyd, as medium, to both of whom he pays his tribute in his essay, already noticed, 'My Conviction of the Truth'. He would also have recorded the extent of his obligation to the Church of The Spiritualist National Union, at York Road, Exeter; to the Exeter Branch of the Churches' Fellowship for Psychical and Spiritual Studies; to the College of Psychic Science; and to Mr. Maurice Barbanell, under whose editorship various spiritualistic contributions of his were published; as also to the editors of *Folklore*, and, could he have foreseen the two posthumous articles, of *Light*.

He would have paid his tribute to Miss Olivia Mordue, to whom he directed that this book should be dedicated, for so assiduously urging on its composition and for procuring for him books on the subject. In matters of folklore he owed much to his long association with the Folklore Section of The Devonshire Association and in particular to the conversation, writings and encouragement of Miss Theo Brown.

Among his primary obligations are those to the authorities already mentioned in this Introduction: Erwin Rohde, F.W. H. Myers, Mrs. Stobart, and Professor E. R. Dodds. Among his papers are many transcriptions from the work of all these; and also from E. J. Dingwall's *Ghosts and Spirits in the Ancient World* (London 1930) and Franz Cumont's *After Life in Roman Paganism* (New Haven, U.S.A. 1922). I should also include Mr. R. T. Rundle Clark, whose fascinating *Myth and Symbol in Ancient Egypt* was on his shelves, and with whom he had enjoyed the privilege of conversation. My own debt to Mr. Rundle Clark will be apparent (pp. 179–82).

He was particularly impressed by J. D. Unwin's *Sex and Culture* (London 1934) to which he refers often in his *Folklore* article, already noticed, 'Origins of Belief'. He talked to me of it, and made extended transcriptions. Its influence may have been stronger than our present annotations indicate; and so may Dingwall's. He used C. E. Vulliamy's *Immortal Man: a Study of Funeral Customs and of Beliefs in regard to the Nature*

B

and Fate of the Soul (London 1926), and from it printed a long quotation in his *Folklore* article, 'The After-Life in Greek and Roman Antiquity', recording (*Folklore* 69, December 1958; p. 235, note 24) that both it and Mrs. Stobart's volume were brought to his notice by Miss Mordue. Other names, mentioned in this article, which might be added, are: Henri Frankfort, G. Rachel Levy and W. J. Perry. Two notable spiritualistic books mentioned in 'My Conviction of the Truth' are: the Rev. Maurice Elliott's *The Psychic Life of Jesus* (London 1938) and Major Alan Howgrave-Graham's *The Dead Companions* (London 1950). To all authorities of classical learning mentioned in our notes, if such authorities are dated before 1964, he may be assumed to have been indebted.

To my own helpers my gratitude is unbounded. My first was my brother's friend of the University of Exeter, Mr. Hugh Stubbs, who went twice through the text, noting errors and suggesting adjustments. He made out for me many pages of critical annotation; to some important points he devoted a personal research; and his early encouragement was a strong support. I was fortunate to have such stores of classical knowledge as his at my disposal.

At first we expected to remain content with few references to authorities, concentrating only on finding line references for actual quotations or points of peculiar importance from classical authors. For these I had the assistance of Mr. Raymond J. Clark, another friend of my brother's (recently appointed to a lectureship in Classics at the University of St. John's, Newfoundland), who found time from his Ph.D. researches at Exeter to do what was required. He did far more than I had expected. Not only did he trace the sources of many statements which could, though less satisfactorily, have been allowed to stand unsupported, but he added also many references to modern commentators. He spent many long sessions with me, discussing details and clearing my mind of confusion.

Most of Mr. Stubbs' contributions are, by their very nature, now embedded in our text. Nearly all the bracketed line and section references to classical authors within the text are Mr. Clark's; and so are the references in the footnotes, in so far as they apply to classical authors or commentaries upon them by modern scholars. For the rest the material in the notes, with all matters therein of general argument and references to modern, non-classical writers, and including the long discussion of Egyptian Spiritualism on pp. 179–82, is my own. Where there is some particular reason to credit an argument to its author, I have added initials. I might here add that Mr. Stubbs directed me to Reynolds and Charlton's book on Arthur Machen referred to on p. 186 and to the Hebraic encyclopaedias of p. 198.

Last, I handed the complete work over to Mr. John D. Christie of the University of Glasgow, general editor of my brother's posthumous works, who has already brought out the volumes *Vergil: Epic and Anthropology* (1967) and *Many-Minded Homer* (1968). Before that my brother had for many years relied on his unique editorial powers. Mr. Christie had helped us at an earlier stage of *Elysion*, pointing to imperfections that were escaping notice. He has now undertaken a final and exhaustive revision. To it he has brought all his meticulous scholarship and instinct for consistency of detail and exactitude of expression. He discovered among my brother's papers and publications important items to amplify or supplement our material, and has suggested major structural rearrangements to clarify the argument. There must be few, if any, living scholars with such a flair for the solving of problems and so lynx-like an eye for the detection of faults. Those, and there are many, who have enjoyed the benefit of his help will understand the nature and extent of my good fortune.

We wish to express our gratitude to Miss Betty Knott of Glasgow University, who at a late stage read our typescript and offered valuable suggestions. For our note on the game Hopscotch (p. 193 below) we are indebted to Mr. Peter L. Cavacciolo. I would like to record that my own spiritualistic experience has been enriched, as was my brother's, by frequent attendances at the circle of Dorothy Perkins, now Mrs. Harold Grainger, in Exeter.

In inserting the dates of ancient authors Mr. Raymond Clark has, with a very few exceptions, followed the *Oxford Classical Dictionary*. A volume often occurring in our notes is: H. Diels, *Die Fragmente der Vorsokratiker*, 5th, 6th and 7th eds., edited with additions by W. Kranz (Berlin 1934–54). To this we refer simply as: Diels-Kranz. Volume numerals for journals are given in Arabic, but for books in Roman. Page references only carry the letter 'p.' when referring to our own text.

Finally, I wish to draw attention to two works of importance to those interested in the more general problems raised in both this Introduction and the following pages. The first is Edward Carpenter's *The Drama of Love and Death* (London 1912), to which some of my notes refer. The second is Mr. D. Shaw's biographical account, at present in preparation, of that remarkable thinker of the last century, Gerald Massey (see my note on pp. 181–2 below).

For permission to print on our title-page the quotation from *Little Gidding* I am indebted to Mrs. Valerie Eliot.

Exeter, January 1970   G.W.K.

ADDITIONAL NOTE

Certain specific adjustments should here be recorded.

The section on Vergil has already been used in the volume of Vergilian essays edited by Professor D. R. Dudley in the series *Studies in Latin Literature and its Influence* (1969). In our present text the sentence on Nautes (p. 137), which appears in the other version as my brother wrote it, I have reworded to correspond more closely with his own translation of the *Aeneid*.

On pp. 85–6 we quote a translation made by my brother and found among his papers in order to supplement his discussion of Pindar's Elysion. On p. 88 I have inserted a line or two of my own on Euripides, who seemed to deserve a place beside Aeschylus and Sophocles. On p. 159 we support the author's remarks on Tertullian by a reference to Norman J. Bull's *The Rise of the Church* and also by an extended quotation from Tertullian's *De Anima*, which would have been in his mind as he had drawn elsewhere on Arthur Findlay's *The Psychic Stream*, where the passage is quoted. On p. 124 I have, in response to Mr. Christie's observation that our text seemed to give Horace too much credit for a thought on death earlier and better expressed by Catullus, decided to quote the actual Latin of the latter's sad and beautiful lines. My brother's discussion (p. 152) of St. Paul's statements on resurrection, relating them to a reading of 'the last trump' as applying originally to an individual's death, was cramped and needed re-wording and expansion. There are other adjustments, and the occasional small addition: on p. 49 we lengthen a sentence to clarify a difficult transition. Our only major expansion occurs in the treatment of Marjorie Livingston's *The New Nuctemeron* on pp. 155-8. The original account was rather brief for a work so important in our context. Among my brother's papers I found his notes on it, with transcriptions of passages, some of which I have incorporated; and in reading the book itself for purposes of checking I have drawn on it yet further. The results may now be, and read like, an interpretative exposition of my own. For the rest, wherever adjustments have been needed, I have done what I could to preserve the tone and wavelength of my brother's style.

All the material, manuscripts, typescripts, and various re-typings, will be preserved in the Library of the University of Exeter.

I   *Tradition and Folklore*

The beliefs of classical antiquity grow out of the matrix of world-beliefs. They, strangely, evince a certain similarity, a certain uniformity. Yet the indications are scattered enough in both space and time; all over the world, and far back into pre-palaeolithic ages of man. Throughout this vast extent there are indications of a belief that death is not the end for men or animals.

Matter and mind are much the same everywhere on this earth. Early Man had apparently some ways of looking at both which were universal to him but seem strange to us. But reason has always been there, it has always been free, and it has always been reason. The procedure has been to note what is experience and to express it in communication. But experience varies according to interests; people may miss things which seem obvious to others. And descriptions and reactions depend on all sorts of conditions, including the multitudinously different conceptions of what is possible and what is likely. A traditional background weighs heavily on those who belong to it. Custom is king. Clear right interpretations may become strangely difficult to suggest or to accept after many generations have strengthened habits. All minds run in grooves. The grooves get deeper, and it becomes harder to see over the sides. The dead have always become spirits at death, and so far as we can make out have been seen as ghosts by some members of all peoples at all times. But what has been thought, said and done about them has been various, even extravagantly various. Ghosts have strange qualities and powers. It has been unusual to doubt their existence. But almost any theory of them must involve apparent impossibilities. And, when choosing between apparent impossibilities, even good reasoning powers are handicapped. Tradition then easily takes control.

There are, of course, blank spaces, with no evidence. But except among the Jews there was little disbelief in survival anywhere or at any time until the Greeks initiated a scepticism in this matter. Since then, this scepticism has sometimes spread considerably. The Sadducees held that there was no resurrection; but even many of the earlier Jews believed in Sheol, a dreary underworld, perhaps derived from Babylonia, and resembling the Hades imagined by Homer and other Greeks. In India the Upanishads recognise survival; and the extreme theories of depersonalised dead are not very early, 'Nirvana' being nearer philosophy than folk-belief. The tendency to deny an after-life is probably more extensive among modern Europeans than ever before. Many adherents of Christianity and other religions which prescribe a belief in survival remain doubtful. Physical scientists are easily led to this same doubt, or indeed to emphatic denials.

For prehistoric times it is normally necessary to try to combine evidence from archaeology with evidence from anthropology. Archaeological remains are compared with the survivals of ancient practice and belief observed today among backward or pre-civilised societies. The easiest way to understand how Stonehenge was erected is to watch modern builders in Assam handling gigantic stones.

But the simplest, and apparently the oldest, evidence hardly needs any comparison. Grave-offerings have been found in graves at least 200,000 years old in East Africa. It is possible that finds twice as old, left by Neanderthal man and perhaps even by Sinanthropus far earlier still, may indicate a belief in survival not only for human beings but also for animals.

The great majority of human beings has believed in survival.

Animals seem to see ghosts, animal and human, as human beings seem to see ghosts, and often enough even more sensitively. Indeed, this sensitivity is in general keener among the less developed human societies. There is not very much of it among ourselves; there was not very much in Periclean Athens. There is far more among the Bornese, the Andaman Islanders, the Australian Aborigines and the Bushmen of the Kalahari Desert, all these being stone-age survivals of very early-type culture. There is great sensitivity among many other peoples, but on the whole less according as their cultural development is more advanced: the more advanced the culture, the less the sensitivity. It is sometimes thought that an increase in intellectual activity weakens it.

People almost everywhere and almost always have believed that some of them, or all of them, survive death and live on as spirits or ghosts. Sir James Frazer, challenged on his perhaps excessive attention to tree-cults, replied that on the whole he thought that regard for the dead is the strongest factor in the origin of religion. That can be taken as true, with the reservation that man may also have some intuitive knowledge of the true divine besides his knowledge gained from ghosts. It is sufficient now to consider the ghosts only.

There are many varieties and many complications. But the basis is simple. The dead are believed to exist and to be able to affect the living. They may be loved and trusted or they may be feared. They seem to be feared principally because their mobility gives them great freedom. They are normally more feared than loved, and the treatment given to them is mainly meant either to resist their return or to mollify their expected resentments. Some peoples even violently mourn a dying man to make sure that before he is dead he may be forced to see how sorry his friends are to lose him.

There have been peoples who thought, or think, survival selective, for the nobility only, not for every one. This belief is hard to discuss. Perhaps it is not among the earliest beliefs, but a comparatively late deviation.[1]

In general mankind has not thought that the earthly world and the spirit-world are sharply separated. There are examples of a conviction that babies are conceived when a woman passes a place where the spirit of an ancestor happens to be, and this spirit enters into her, to be reincarnated in her child. The belief in reincarnation is anything but rare: it has been described as universally held by humanity except for a comparatively small section, that is, modern Europeans, and only those among them who are not poets. Further, human spirits have often been supposed to become reincarnated in animal bodies; in pre-civilised thought there is no great distinction between human beings and animals. An animal may be honoured as the first ancestor of a human tribe.

Myths normally belong to places, and this is true of death-myths. The spirits of the dead are said to go to actual, visible places, by actual visible ways. They may be thought to go to a near-by volcano, and dance in the crater, or to some real island to the westward, or down into the earth, and back again when they so wish, through a real, known cave or other orifice in the earth's surface.

The variety is important. There are here two main classes of death-myth. The dead have been thought by many to go to a home below the earth, or they have been thought to journey to the West, usually across the sea or a river, perhaps in search of the sunset, for which in some places a volcano is taken as a substitute.[2] They may be thought simply to survive in their grave. Or they may be supposed certainly to survive, but not in any particular place. As speculation develops, heaven, and sometimes hell also, are imagined above the earth, in or above the earth's atmosphere, and even on or amid the planets and stars or on the sun and moon. But the illogical composite opinion, that the dead survive in the earth and also in a happy land above ground, frequently in the West, is common enough to be called typical.

Eschatological beliefs easily become superstitions, but they are based on observed facts and reasoned argument from those facts. But the facts are often hard or impossible to reconcile with each other. Therefore the observer who reasons from them is compelled to choose between apparent impossibilities. The result is the best that could be done without further knowledge in this or some other field of enquiry. To explain thunder and lightning as fireworks made by a sky-god who throws thunderbolts or stone axes may seem far-fetched, but when no one knew any physics or chemistry no better explanation of an electrical phenomenon could fairly be expected.

Observation of ghosts has been almost universal, and their behaviour and abilities have seemed fairly uniform. Ghosts have above all greater mobility than men living the normal earth-life. Their mobility is so great that it alone can scarcely be discussed without apparent absurdities. They seem to defy the known laws of nature. At least, they live in a world of their own, which is however in contact with this world and somehow in it. But the natural laws of the two worlds are different. In one, legs are needed in order to move, in the other they are not. Any theory must involve a choice between seeming impossibilities.

It was, of course, a very practical matter. Granted the great mobility of ghosts, and also certain observed acts of mischief done by them, it became of great importance to arrange for protection against them. This has been for many people one of the main concerns of their life. Everything depended on mollifying the ghosts, keeping out of their way, or somehow, though this was difficult, coercing them. The need has often seemed urgent or even paramount, and in this urgency an accurate choice between competing theories, all seemingly impossible, was much to expect.

So much is certain, and may reasonably be accepted by most people, unless there are still many people who think there is no such being as a ghost. There are certainly many now, though the number is decreasing, who do not believe that the supposed dead communicate with the living who are still in this earthly world. This disbelief is possible for those who have not considered the evidence, and is, I suppose, just possible for some who have, but only just. The earth goes round the sun. Lightning is due to electric potentials. Ghosts are seen and heard and communicate with the living. These propositions are equally true and can all be denied. 'The village that voted the earth was flat' is not unimaginable.

Ghosts are seen and heard, and are known to do harm, and sometimes good. They also sometimes say what they think and are understood. They even describe the life they lead in their present home and its conditions. When ancient Egyptians, Greeks, and others also, tell stories about life in Heaven, Amentet, or the Isles of the Blessed, or anywhere else, it cannot be assumed that the stories are not based on the report of someone who has been there.

The normal human evidence, therefore, for the life lived after death is a set of facts, some known directly and some indirectly. Sooner or later philosophy begins work on the facts. But long before that they have been collected and retained in folklore. This folklore is not to be disparaged. It may claim some of the praise whimsically given to fairy tales by Chesterton. They, he said, are composed by a number of people, in successive generations, most of whom are sane, whereas books on the other hand are written by single individuals, nearly all of whom are mad. The grain of truth in this is a certain freedom enjoyed by the unlettered. The highly educated have urgent theoretical loyalties. They may easily deny plain fact because in their opinion no man of education would believe such nonsense. Or they may adhere to a school of thought, and subscribe to a system. If so, they may soon judge facts by two criteria instead of one. They may ask what the evidence is, which is correct. They will also ask whether the offered fact fits their system; which is incorrect because irrelevant; it only becomes relevant after a fact has been established as a fact, or in other and different circumstances, when there is no hope of proving a fact, but only of provisionally accepting a probability. Such irrelevant and incorrect judgement happens all the time, as if by instinct. It might be called a necessary part of the myth by which civilised men live. But folklore retains its advantage.

If we imagine an unlettered tribal society or village community with little urban contact, we can soon see that bitter necessity forces the members to accept many facts to them inexplicable, whether or not they fit any theory. That is, they are less prevented by respect for impossibility from accepting the evidence of their eyes and ears. There is plenty of error. But fact is never far away in the background. Indeed, the simple peasants may be nearer than their betters to a correct system, because they will not have discarded good evidence in deference to an incomplete or incorrect system. They are readier for the advance in knowledge which will one day shew that an observed fact which seems impossible is not impossible after all.

However, the peasant is not quite free. His own inferences from facts may well lead to plenty of trouble. And he is almost sure to be subject to some peremptory leadership. Witchdoctors and witches are regularly believed and followed. They are not, of course, always high-minded, unselfish, or even honest. Some are shams. But on the whole it pays them to produce results. And no doubt many of them are fine people with access to much deep truth which they use for the good of others.

The validity of much folklore, however large the proportion of ignorant superstition there may be in it, is well enough known. There may be nothing in the fear of walking under a ladder. Homoeopathic magic seems to be founded on a mistake. But many of the cures work. The point now, however, is none of these; the subject is ghosts. They are often seen by pre-civilised or tribal people, especially by their witch-doctors and witches, whose primary qualification is usually their clairvoyance, their second-sight, often with associated gifts, such as trance-mediumship. No one, therefore, is likely to belittle the ghosts. The people see them. Their leaders see them, if possible still more. The people depend on the leaders for knowing how to keep safe from the ghosts. The leaders may come out of it a little too well. But there is community of purpose and a consent to admit these, and other, facts.

The pity is that near the heart of human things is a propensity to exaggerate, and to want quick and sure results; and other propensities too, not irrelevant here but too complicated for much attention to be given them now. To simplify the matter, mankind has normally feared the ghosts, the spirits of the dead, too much. Some are mischievous, and even dangerous, especially those who have died by suicide or unjust violence. The un-animity of mankind, ancient and modern, about these classes is impressive. But other ghosts are kind and benevolent and can be called good angels. This benevolent class appears to have been underestimated. Sometimes but not always the reason may be simply that those who are not dangerous can be forgotten; sometimes that knowledge is insufficient through failure to enquire into the brighter and more normal side of the after-life; and sometimes because the particular ghosts encountered by many tribes and other groups have in fact not been prepon-derantly good-natured. The last of these possible reasons is important, and indeed tragic. It was known in antiquity, and is known now, that in mental and emotional relationships like attracts like. There have been societies which have been inclined to dismal, pessimistic, spiteful and violent moods. Such moods make it easier for the malevolent spirits and harder for the benevolent spirits to approach. Further, those who have this less positive outlook in life are likely to have it also after death. Thus a society tends to fill some region of the other world with spirits sharing its qualities and preponderant moods: as in Vergil's famous *quisque suos patimur manes*, 'each of us finds the world of death fitted for himself' (*Aeneid* vi, 743). Life, here, is thus more important than it seems to many. It is all the time helping to create the life that will be lived in the beyond. This is a great consolation and one of the reasons why apparent failure in this life is often in effect a triumphant victory with more than earthly value.

These discursive remarks are unavoidable here. It is necessary to be undeceived when different people, even cognate people living near together, have different beliefs and practices concerning the other world. Probably enough they are thinking of different parts of it, with different inhabitants.

Pre-civilised people are normally familiar with ghosts or visible spirits. They are used to seeing them walk about the earth. They find nothing strange in a home above ground for them, perhaps in some different country from which the tribe is thought to have originally come. This place, this home, however, is apparently most often in the West. The dead go the way of the sun; where it goes to rest, they go to rest. But there is also the other view, that the dead go and live below the surface of the earth. The reason is that from a very remote antiquity, hundreds of thousands of years ago, the custom has been to bury dead bodies underground, in the hut where the living dwell or elsewhere. The question to be faced or evaded is the question whether the spirit or soul stays with the body or goes off elsewhere. Funerary offerings are normally put with the body. That is, the soul or spirit is either expected to stay with the body or, if it leaves it, to return to it. Egyptian kings after death revisited their tombs. Alternatively, the offerings may be meant only for immediate use, during the journey to a land of the dead elsewhere. But in any case the belief in an underworld-home of the dead has often been made explicit in myth. It is a traditional belief, clearly described in speech, and later in poetry. Such was the doctrine of the Sumerians and Babylonians, at the beginning of civilisation, and of some Jews and some Greeks also. The dead were thought to survive in a dim half-life, with little strength and little mind, for a long time, or for ever.

Right at the start of literature, in the Babylonian epic *Gilgamesh*, there is a séance,[1] and the spirit of Enkidu appears and speaks depressingly of the life beyond. Gilgamesh himself sails over the waters of death to meet Ut-napishtim, a kind of Noah who alone had a true eternal life. Gilgamesh, seeking eternal life for himself, failed to gain it.

The story of Ut-napishtim—but the correct spelling may be very different—is, if not the first, at least the most explicit among early indications of a kind of heaven, a happy land reserved for some of the dead. Ut-napishtim and his wife were specially favoured. The Gods liked them. Before them, perhaps for half a million years, the tenuous evidence suggests that the future life was imagined as active and very tolerable, often in a series of reincarnations in human or animal bodies. Early Egyptian burials, at about the same time, a little after or before 3000 B.C., as the earliest versions of the *Epic of Gilgamesh*, probably imply that the later Egyptian belief was already held—that the Pharaoh and perhaps others went to Amentet, 'the West', in the boat of the sun, and lived below the ground in a bright underworld, very like the Egyptian earthly world, where all the joys of life were available, and the fish jumped of their own accord into the fisherman's basket. No thought of reincarnation has been proved for Egypt, which is strange since later the Greeks attributed this doctrine to Egypt; nor has it been proved for Babylonia. The Egyptian pattern of a journey to the West and the residence in an underworld heaven has been thought the origin of this pattern wherever else it occurs. The Egyptians also communicated with the dead mediumistically. The evidence is inescapable, but we still find many high authorities maintaining that they did nothing of the kind.[2]

In the great civilisations from which the Greeks learnt or could have learnt, the dead were buried with honour, especially, but not only, the royal dead. They were carefully equipped for their future life. In Sumeria, and originally perhaps in Egypt too, slaves or others were sacrificed to attend their master. As usual among mankind, a future life was expected either for all the dead or for some of them; perhaps at first for some, and later, by a gradual extension, for all. Burial was in structures or excavations in or on, or in and on, the earth. The Sumerians and Babylonians imagined a dreary Hades below the earth where souls lived on. So did some of the Hebrews. The Greeks believed in such a Hades. They may have learnt to do so from Asiatics. But the Celts may once have had a similar belief. If so, the Greeks may have inherited this conception from their common ancestors. The Egyptians, by contrast, had a strong faith in a heaven for the Good, who were thought to live a happy life of enjoyment under the earth, or in a western land, where conditions were as they are in mortal life but without any of the disadvantages. Some Greeks from early times believed in such a heaven for some people. What the Minoans believed is obscure. That they hoped for a heaven has been suggested, but is rather probable than certain. They buried the dead with care. Embalming is a notably Egyptian practice. It was known and apparently practised in the other great areas of ancient civilisation, but not, it seems, carried very far in any except Egypt.

Within the clear general pattern the variety is great. All people may survive, or only the nobility, perhaps only royalty. They may have a happy or a dull after-life. They may be mainly loved and trusted, or mainly feared—if not indeed hated. They may or may not be reincarnated, either in human or animal bodies, but reincarnation is usually expected. The beliefs are coloured by local geography. To the Eskimo Hades is icy and wet, but not so to others.

Pre-civilised people have to conform to tribal customs. The discipline, especially at initiations, sustains uniformity. Sin is mainly damage done by supposed black magic. Normally, the magician and the sinner are detected by a witch-doctor, and punished. Rewards and punishments after death are usually considered to be a rather late notion. But in early Egypt it is said that the dying were always taught a 'negative confession', which they were to make after death, before Gods in Judgement, specifically disclaiming a list of sins. The negative confession has often been discounted, as though the purpose had been magical and no one was ever really so innocent. The truth seems to be that the Egyptians really did maintain a high standard of morality, and the negative confession was on the whole sincere and true.[3]

Nothing has been said so far about any heaven in the sky. This notion mainly belongs to later classical antiquity. Then a tendency appears, and grows, towards localising all the dead in the air or sky, even those in Hades. The reason for doing this lay perhaps mainly in cosmological difficulties. Plato's variety of myths amusingly shews how hard it was to find a satisfactory and credible place to put all the dead in their very different degrees of merit. But the origin of the notion can be pushed much farther back. It is probable enough that the sun and moon counted as divinities long ago in the stone ages. Sumerian monarchs were identified with them, the king as the sun and the queen as the moon or, strangely, the king as the moon and the queen as the sun. Egyptian monarchs were not only bulls but also bulls as pictured by bull-shaped constellations in the sky. The starry crown of Ariadne, translated to the sky by Dionysus, seems clearly derived from the girdle of Babylonian Ishtar, which was identified in the starry heaven. In nearer Asia during many centuries religious beliefs had been linked with astrology. Early cultures were oddly capable of depth on depth of multiple identification. Certainly the Babylonians and Egyptians were philosophically quite at home in the sky. If a king can, besides much else, be Horus, a hawk, a bull, a throne, and a constellation, the spirit of a man might easily live on, under, and above the earth. If each man, further, had his astrological place in the Zodiac while alive on earth, the conception of a sky-heaven presents no aspect of unlikelihood. Certainly the late classical thinkers and mystics need not surprise us when they long to take flight from the prison of earth and live near the stars, whose divine order they revered, and God Himself, whom they worshipped and adored.

The matrix from which classical thought grew and emerged

belongs to the world of a few thousand years ago. Much in that world was then already very old, including some thoughts and beliefs; but they are hard to identify when there are no written documents. This is where modern comparisons can help, and help in opening another window on the background of classical eschatology. The window is offered by 'shamans' and 'shamanism', dancing wizards or medicine men or prophets, who have been found and investigated during the last three generations among hunting tribes, especially in Siberia.[4] There a number of shamans have allowed European anthropologists not only to watch them perform but also hear their own accounts of operations and experiences. Dancing is important because it starts their trances, in which they have abnormal powers and vision. A shaman becomes, it is said, 'dissociated'. Or his soul goes away on astral travel. He, or it, may even reach 'the sixteenth heaven'. The trance passes, and the shaman can then reveal to his congregation what he has seen or learnt. It may be a truth about the origin of the world, or some simple but useful answer to a problem of daily life. Similar proficiency is found elsewhere, especially among the Eskimos. It has been suggested that shamanistic performances succeed more easily in a northern climate.

Shamans of today do not immediately prove anything about pre-Greek beliefs. But a comparison can make them usefully suggestive. The present-day northern hunters are very like the palaeolithic hunters who left their drawings in French and Spanish caves. There is actually a convincing shaman there pictured.[5] Among other evidence are signs that the old hunters carried out a sacrifice very much as the Ainu of Japan carry out their famous bear-sacrifice still. It is hardly a matter of proof. But it becomes extremely likely that many thousands of years ago hunting tribes had their shamans who travelled in trance to other spheres or other planes of being, perhaps even to a 'sixteenth heaven', and, like the subject of an experiment which we shall presently be discussing (pp. 72 and 94 below), came back, and 'reported each thing'.

There is a very remarkable report from a Siberian shaman who in trance saw strange visions of human and animal creatures contributing to the world-process and controlling the origins and destinies of men and the machinery of reincarnation. It is clearly of the same class as Plato's 'Myth of Er' in the *Republic* (x, 614 B ff.), where Er the Armenian, left for dead on a battlefield, revived and reported on the background of human life and the divine destiny which controls it. Such supposed trance-visits to the beyond may or may not have happened in the Old Stone Age; but it is practically certain that they frequently happened long before the historical emergence of the Greeks and Romans.

Such, at least, is one origin for beliefs about the other world. People went there in trance, or in thought, or only said that they did. But at least some, even if mistaken, were hardly lying, in view of the many modern cases of what is known as 'astral travel',[6] in which the honesty of the 'travellers' is not in doubt. If so, many prophets of whatever kind must surely have enriched humanity's conception of a life beyond by the reports of their dreams or visions. It is perhaps admissible to think that true mystic experiences also occurred in the distant past as they have occurred nearer to, and in, our own time.

On the whole, the possibility of mystical experience is widely recognised both by those who hold, and those who do not hold, established religious beliefs. Less widely recognised are the possibilities of astral travel by the soul of a magician or prophet in trance and of clairvoyant perception of another world than ours. There is, however, no doubt whatever that people have believed in all this, many people, at many times and in many places. Even if the most wonderful thing that really happens is just an occasional dream or nightmare, it will still be true to assert that conceptions of an after-life, of a world beyond death, have often been based on, or modified by, the experiences of minds released from, or active beyond, the limitations of normal daylight consciousness. As for dreams, they are frankly recognised by pre-civilised peoples both in Asia and America to be an authoritative source for religious rituals. A North American Indian might dream a ritual and perform it, or else sell the dream-directions to another, only the dreamer himself or a buyer having the right to use them.

3 Greeks: Introductory

The Greeks shared universal human experience, but some of them tried much harder than most other people to reason from experience. They even, or some of them, achieved a supremely reasonable account of spirits and the life after death. But it was nothing like a nation-wide and generally accepted system. Truth is stranger than fiction, and it is proper that it should be. Fiction is what comes naturally; people easily invent it out of well-known elements of experience, and it fits in with the assumptions and expectations of other people. Truth, or rather any new truth, is just what people did not know before and is not what they were expecting.

The Greeks tried many schemes for explaining the movements of the sun, moon and stars. Apparently only Aristarchus of Samos (c. 310–230 B.C.) found the right answer.

He suggested that the stars are fixed, and the earth and the other planets go round the sun. This simple and now obvious truth, the only one among many theories not open to the strongest objections, was quickly rejected, and no more is heard of it, except that Cleanthes (c. 331–232 B.C.), the religious philosopher famous for his hymn to Zeus, threatened to prosecute Aristarchus for impiety. It took a long struggle to establish this simple truth. Tradition was against it, and, though, being true, it must certainly be possible, the impossibility of opposite theories no doubt seemed no more impossible than the apparent impossibility of the right explanation.

Ghosts and spirits have presented a puzzle too, and it has

taken a long struggle to reach, and to recommend effectively
to a large number of people, what now seems to those who
take an interest in this matter, if not exactly a simple and obvious
truth, though that is what it seems to many, at least an undeniable
certainty. In Latin classical antiquity several writers left documents shewing that the best and most reasonable ancient and
modern views are much alike.

The Greeks did not begin in a vacuum. They brought their
own original culture, some of which they shared with ancestors
of Celts and Teutons, from wherever they came from, perhaps
east-central Europe or south Russia. But when they appear in
history they had already learnt from Asiatic, Egyptian, and
Minoan civilisation.

The Greek and Roman phase of history shews its first sign
in the appearance of an Indo-European name in southern Asia
Minor at or soon after 2600 B.C. But it is not till a little after
2000 B.C. that the arrival of numerous speakers of Indo-European
languages in southern lands really begins. There are hints that an
early form of Greek may have been spoken in Greece a century
or so before then. But the establishment of states by these northern invaders can be dated in India and Asia Minor at about 1800–
1700 B.C. and in Greece about 1650 B.C. In Italy the date is a little
later. To India came the Aryans, to Asia Minor and the great
river plains beyond came Kassites, Luvians, Hurrians and Hittites,
to Greece the Greeks, and to Italy the Latins and their kindred.
Unlike the others, the Greeks and Latins had nothing to say
about themselves, at least to us, for many centuries after their
first arrival, so that our names for them are more general
than detailed.

The Greeks appear out of a more ancient world, and they themselves emerge from a larger aggregation of peoples and tribes,
a matrix within a matrix. The Indo-European speakers are a
special, and up-to-date, element among the ancient, pre-classical,
peoples. They brought with them a new breath of air. They
were, above all, charioteers. They had horses, and used them,
having a mental vigour to match speed in locomotion. They

also were now in having, and handling, their languages. There is a famous correspondence, the Tell el-Amarna Letters between the Egyptian Pharaoh Akhenaten and a Hittite king.[1] The Egyptian letters are formal and archaic and shew the stiff formality of an old-fashioned language. The Hittite writer writes in balanced structures, flexibly reviewing together different considerations, and producing a result more like Ciceronian periods, or modern business letters, than the priestly formalities of antique style.

What the Northerners, including ancestors of the Greeks, thought about the after-life, in so far as it is known, does not amount to very much. Some remains in south Russia and near the lower Danube attributed to what is called the Kurgan Culture may be theirs. There are mound-burials with offerings, at least indicating the basic minimum, a belief in survival. The passage of the Indo-European speakers has not been exactly traced. But, when they arrived in central and southern Greece, they soon left their vigorous and enduring imprint in their Mycenaean remains.

Before they came, Greece had been sparsely occupied by a rather dull neolithic population, with normal neolithic culture. Again there are some grave-offerings. But they seem to have been preceded a few generations earlier by a mysterious inroad from Asia Minor, testified by place-names such as Athenae, Parnassos, Cephissos, and Corinthos; and a few common nouns such as *asaminthos*, 'bath'. These un-Greek name-terminations belong to Asia Minor and seem to have been introduced into Greece a little before 2000 B.C. The invaders give an impression of a short-lived occupation. They left place-names, and disappeared—rather like the Franks, who invaded France, gave France its name, and vanished from history.

Then, about 1700, the Mycenaeans appear. Signs of previous Greek occupation, or visitation, have been found. It is argued that some Greek words were used in Greece before 2000 B.C. If this is a fact, it remains mysterious. Even the Mycenaeans were not so long ago mysterious. Some said they were Minoans from Crete, occupying Greece. But arguments published in the 1930s suggested that the Mycenaeans were indeed Greeks, though Greeks with a style of expression very different from the style of the full historic Greek period, a thousand years or so later. The matter was settled when over six hundred inscribed clay tablets, found at Pylos in 1939, were deciphered in 1952, and shewn to be written in an early form of Greek. Their date is about 1220 B.C. They are associated with the very fine Mycenaean palace at Pylos. There is no room for doubt that the Mycenaeans spoke Greek, and were Greeks.

However it happened, the Mycenaeans were Greeks, but influenced apparently by the Minoan art which had preceded theirs in Greek lands. Perhaps Minoan artists were persuaded by the Mycenaean Greeks to work for them and to teach them; though they do not cease to be themselves, in contrast with the Minoans, and they had their own burials. The Minoans laid the dead to rest in small chambers cut in rock, sometimes in a rock-face. The Mycenaeans elaborated burial, especially royal burial in their famous Beehive Tombs. There the whole apparatus is rich, artistic, and spacious. It might almost, but not quite, compete with the supreme elaborations of Sumer and Egypt, being perhaps only inferior to Tutankhamen's grave furniture in quantity rather than perfection.

The Minoans are to us reticent concerning the after-life. They believed in it. But it is hard to extract any declaration about it from their art. The most hopeful by far of their monuments, if it is one of theirs, is the famous Hagia Triadha Sarcophagus.[2] It is unique, and indeed may not be, strictly, Minoan at all. It comes from southern Crete and is dated, usually, at about 1700 B.C. At this date some mysterious invaders from Asia Minor were perhaps occupying the east of the island. At any rate, the richly painted scene on it is certainly a funeral ceremony. A procession moves towards a door, in which stands a figure. The participants are making offerings to the dead man conceived as living still and standing up within his rock tomb.

Both the Minoans and the Mycenaeans have left rich artistic representations including many figures, some human, and some part human and part animal. Some may well be demons or protective deities or death-gods. Many have been boldly or indeed brilliantly interpreted. But more certainty is needed. One representation is lavish in detail, but again doubtful. This is the celebrated 'Ring of Nestor', a gem picked up in Greece in 1894.³ On it is a field quartered by a cross from side to side both ways, like a hot cross-bun. The cross has been taken to be either a 'world tree' like the northern Yggdrasil, or two rivers, intersecting, in the underworld. Among the other details are a welcoming goddess, and the soul—as afterwards in Greece and elsewhere—shewn as a butterfly. If this is true, or approximately true, here is the first Greek heaven, or Elysion, already imagined and pictured in Mycenaean times, when many Greek myths certainly originated. Whenever this heaven may have been first conceived, it continued. It is assumed by Homer (*c.* 800 B.C.) and Hesiod (*c.* 750 B.C.), and remains a resource in literature afterwards. The name Elysion already existed when their poems were composed.

The tribes and races of the world have varied in their thoughts of the after-life. Those who are more advanced have often enough believed in a Valhalla or Happy Hunting Ground or an Eden restored. A poetical, and presently a literary, picture is formed, a picture of a blissful life in sunshine amid flowers to go on perhaps for ever. There is the Golden Age past or, as in Isaiah (e.g. XI, 1–10; LXV, 1–25),⁴ to come. Now the picture is available for application in different contexts. It need not be in a different world. It may be in this world, future, past, or now, but somewhere far away; or it may be a world of spirits, men who have lived on earth and died, or who have been translated, like Enoch, without dying.⁵ It might be argued that whatever other people have seriously believed, the ancient Greeks and Romans, when they describe their heaven and indeed their purgatory and their hell, were not simply expressing a religious belief but were building up a fancy from a store of poetic material. But the other view, that at least sometimes they expressed a genuine, perhaps even an authenticated, belief may well turn out to be more probable.

The Greeks, when they begin to appear in a history of their own after the destruction of their own early Mycenaean culture, that is in the Geometric Age, take a great interest in funerals. The great vases of the Dipylon style dated about 900 B.C. and found in Athens have elaborate pictures of funeral processions in which a dead man is conveyed on a four-horse chariot to his tomb. Not long after, a phase of cremation ensues. The normal practice of mankind has always been inhumation, but often cremation has been practised temporarily. A kind of partial cremation is found in Mycenaean graves; a small part of the body is burnt or singed, for what reason is not yet clear. Now Homer, who means to describe events which we date just before 1200 B.C., always describes, or implies, a full-scale cremation on a funeral pyre. The disagreement is hard to understand. However, there seems to be some archaeological evidence for a very early practice of cremation actually near Troy itself. Homer may be accurate; if so, it is surprising that at about this date there is no other evidence for cremation but strong proof of general inhumation. Otherwise, Homer may have been transferring to his dramatic date, 1200 B.C. or thereabouts, the funeral customs of a later, perhaps of his own, time.[6]

During the rest of classical antiquity inhumation was usual but cremation continues to occur, on the whole sporadically. In Italy, from a very early date, both inhumation and cremation were practised. At all, or nearly all, periods some Romans, but never all of them, cremated their dead. The difference of custom is usually thought to express a difference of belief. Certainly those who believe in the resurrection of the physical body must always decide for inhumation. Those who believe in no resurrection, but either extinction, or a continuous survival of a spirit, detached from the body at, or soon after, death, are at liberty to cremate their dead. The distinction has been considered to be an important difference between Graeco-Roman paganism and Christianity. Paganism believed in spirit survival, but Christianity, and few other contemporary religions besides Persian Zoroastrianism, believed in resurrection.

4   *Homer and Hesiod*

The Homeric Poems, the *Iliad* and the *Odyssey*, were finally made into what they are about 800–750 B.C., when cremation had been going on for some generations and was soon to fall, to some extent, out of favour. In Homer, the dead are cremated and this releases the spirit to go to Hades. Till cremation the other spirits keep the new-comer away, and the spirit of the lately dead, sometimes visible, and recognisable, flits near the body. Such is the condition of the spirit of Patroclus, when it appeals to Achilles for cremation (*Iliad* XXIII, 62 ff.). A kind of embalmment is known. Sarpedon's body is embalmed (*Iliad* XVI, 667–75) so that it may be preserved while it is conveyed home to Lycia for the funeral. Apollo somehow preserves the body of Hector (*Iliad* XXIII, 188 ff.), to keep it until Priam comes to Achilles and is allowed by him to take it back with him to Troy. The body is important. It is cremated, the ashes are put in an urn, the urn is buried, and a large mound of earth is heaped over it (*Iliad* XXIV, 599–601, 777 ff.). Human beings and animals are sacrificed. In Homer, the rites and the offerings are elaborate. Achilles (*Iliad* XXI, 27; XXIII, 175) sacrificed twelve captive Trojans to Patroclus, and horses also, a practice reported among the Scythians of south Russia by Herodotus (*c.* 485–425 B.C.; IV, 72). Presumably there had once been an intention to provide the dead chieftain with servants and animals to use in his new life, but the reason is not mentioned, and may have been forgotten, if not by Achilles, if he ever lived, at least by Homer. The rites for Patroclus include many normal animal-sacrifices,

and also large-scale funeral games with chariot-races and wrest-
ling and other athletic competitions. The meaning of all this
is obscure, in spite of efforts to understand it.

A large part of the twenty-third book of the *Iliad* is devoted
to the funeral of Patroclus and the games that follow. But the
elaboration is less than among the Sumerians, who at Ur seem
to have sacrificed the whole court, at least forty people, with
exquisite jewellery, to attend the dead king: excavation has
established all this, with signs that those who were sacrificed
went willingly, and perhaps were drugged unconscious before
they were killed. In Egypt there was also immense elaboration,
including, according to much of the evidence, many little
figures, Ushabti, 'Answerers', and models, such as models of
boats with their crews, all intended to revive into spiritual
life and activity quite as well as real people and genuinely useful
things could have revived. Human sacrifice may have been
usual originally, and was not altogether abandoned.

There may well have been a forward-looking motive,
derived from the widespread wish to enliven and strengthen
any king or chief, whether dead or alive. Egyptian, and indeed
Chinese, kings had to run fast and plough a furrow, to prove
or enhance their vitality, and to communicate it, fertilisingly, to
the soil.[1] The exhibitions of strength and competence at the
Homeric funeral were perhaps meant to communicate strength
to the reviving spirit of the chief. Some procedures may be
transferred from an earlier part of the chief's life, perhaps from
some inauguration, to his last occasion, his funeral. A divine
king may be chosen because he shewed prowess. In the *Odyssey*
(VIII, 178 ff.) Odysseus competes with Phaeacian princes in
Scheria. He throws a discus further than the others, and offers
to box, wrestle, and shoot. The incident is perhaps out of its
original context.[2] He ought to be winning, by his abilities, a
princess—Nausicaa—and a throne. As it is he proves himself—
and goes home to his Penelope.

Everything, then, is done for Patroclus; and Patroclus says
that he himself must lie buried with Achilles in the same tomb

(*Iliad* XXIII, 83–4). Strangely, there is nothing after, in the *Iliad*. There are no regular grave-offerings nor any entertainment of ancestral spirits at an old Greek All Souls' Day. Such were the practices of later Greeks, and other peoples of course, including the Chinese. Homer, and his characters, want an elaborate funeral. To miss that meant that the spirit would wander, lost; a reason why death at sea might well be specially dreaded, as it used to be in Brittany. But Homeric Greeks passionately loved fame. The high barrow above the urn could be seen from far, and identified, perhaps for a very long time. Homer himself mentions a hero's tomb serving as a landmark and an active memorial to its occupant (*Iliad* VII, 89–90; cf. *Odyssey* XXIV, 80–4). There are however some exceptions in Homer, two in particular.

Menelaus is not to die but to be translated to a kind of Heaven or Elysion (*Odyssey* IV, 561–9). This is not through any merit of his own but simply because he was married to Helen, a daughter of Zeus—and not even as a consolation for the dreadful time which she had given him. The other great heroes, Achilles, Agamemnon and the rest, all went to Hades (*Odyssey* XI, 387–567; for a different tradition concerning Achilles see p. 61 below). Heracles, in a way, had done better still (*Odyssey* XI, 601–4; and see p. 50 below, note). Before Trojan times, after being poisoned through treachery, he died on a funeral pyre which he caused to be lighted to end his misery. He, or his spirit, went to Olympus, where he lived for ever, a God among Gods, married to Hebe, the Goddess of Youth. He was so promoted because he was himself a son of Zeus. He is a unique example. In early times it was next to impossible for even a very great hero to become a God. But four hundred years or less after Homer every Orphic initiate was told 'you shall be a God instead of a mortal'.

Orphism was a 'mystery religion' and a kind of secret religious society, but it, and other 'mystery religions', mainly belong to this later time. It has been thought, however, that Orphism was partly responsible for the other of the two main exceptions in Homer to Homer's normal assumptions.

There is a book (XI) of the *Odyssey* in which Odysseus calls up the spirits of the dead and actually visits Hades. Instructed by Circe, he sails to the West, to a place 'covered with mist and cloud' (*Odyssey* XI, 15). Wherever it was in the real world, if anywhere, it was reached by sailing westward over the sea, as in Sumerian and Egyptian death-beliefs.[3] But the theme of the underground home of the dead is simultaneously preserved, a duplication found in Egypt and elsewhere.

Odysseus wants to ask the prophet Teiresias how he is to find his way home to Ithaca. He calls up the spirit of Teiresias, 'the only one who is rational, the others being all mere flitting shadows' (*Odyssey* X, 494–5). To do this he digs a trench, sacrifices sheep, lets the blood fill the trench, and waits for the spirits to come. They do come, 'the spectres of those who had died, up out of Erebos' (*Odyssey* XI, 37); that is, from deep in the earth which the word 'Erebos' now meant in Greek, though in Semitic languages *ereb* had meant the West:[4] a very condensed example of the combination in a single myth of the two main tenets, that the dead 'go under' or 'go west', the myths having given us these two colloquial expressions.

The Greek language gave Erebos to Homer. But he himself arranged a combination of the myths on a larger scale. He begins with the trench. The spirits come up, and each time Homer says 'And up came the spirit of . . .' But after a while there is a change. We no longer seem to be waiting at the trench above ground but instead to be walking about in Hades, below the surface of the earth, moving from exhibit to exhibit.[5]

The trench ritual is no doubt pre-Homeric, but, apart from certain literary references probably inspired by the *Odyssey*, we meet it again after Homer only in the Athenian festival of the Anthesteria, which included a sort of All Souls' Day. Little insect-like spirits are shewn flying up, shepherded by Hermes, on vase paintings. At the end the Athenians said 'Outside, Spirits! The Anthesteria is over'. In contrast Homer avoids many such already old-fashioned matters, which only come clearly into our view after his time. It is accordingly natural that his narrative should change from the ritual on earth to an apparent walk to and through the underworld.

In several parts of the world there are stories of such journeys, and such returns, because of course one of the main points is that Odysseus, and among others Sumerian Gilgamesh, both went to and returned from another world while still alive in the flesh. The Greeks after Homer had several poems called 'Descents', '*Katabaseis*', which described journeys to the underworld. Some are called 'Orphic' and were part of Orphic doctrine (p. 98 below), and used for the teaching of initiates. Little of this poetry survives; Homer's 'Descent' in the *Odyssey* may, as some have thought, count as an example. In general—and this is perhaps important—the name 'Orphic' has probably been over-applied. The Greeks, among them those who joined the Orphic sect but also many others who were not Orphics, came to have a considerable amount of doctrine, if not indeed information, concerning the after-life. The secret societies specialised in shewing their adherents how to act in view of the facts, that is, how to ensure a happy after-life.

Homer's after-life is not happy. It is, except for a very few, Menelaus, Heracles,[6] and perhaps three or four others, no more than a half-life in a half-light. Certain very great sinners, Tityos, Sisyphus, Tantalus, suffer lasting torments (*Odyssey* XI, 576–600). The vast majority, good or bad, of those who have died just join the throng of feeble spirits. The Homeric Hades was a sad domain where even Achilles could say that he would rather be a serf, the chattel of a master who was himself in no secure possession of an estate and had little to live on, than King over all the mere corpses who are the dead. 'Valiant Odysseus', he says, 'never seek to console me for dying' (*Odyssey* XI, 488–91).

Minos has a privileged place, settling cases and giving judgement among the dead (*Odyssey* XI, 568–71). Elsewhere in Greek mythology Aeacus and Rhadamanthus, the latter mentioned at *Odyssey* IV, 564, were grouped with Minos as judges in the beyond: having been just on earth they are given authority after death. In Vergil's *Aeneid* (VI, 566–9) Rhadamanthus is a judge in the underworld, punishing spirits for their former sins. There appears to be in general some confusion between judgement delivered for former sins and the exercise of judgement, such as that of Homer's Minos, in respect to activities in Hades. It is not easy to see what offences could be committed by Homer's shades after death, for they had neither the initiative nor the opportunity.

The Egyptian who died was immediately faced with judgement. At each gate on his way he had to make his 'negative confession' and declare to the waiting Gods that he had not committed any sin, specifying each sin that he had not committed. Apparently, though the 'confession' was not always quite true, failure was rare. Those who passed went to their bliss. Early Greece knew something of Egypt, but little sign of this knowledge is given. But it is likely that somewhere Greece learnt of this kind of judgement, and reflected this in their appointment of Judges of the Dead, afterwards forgetting and leaving the myth incoherent. Much civilisation lies behind the Greeks. Later a great deal was to be made of this judgement, especially by Plato, and surely there is truth in what was said.

As for the dreary Hades of Homer and many other Greeks, it is like the Sumerian and Babylonian and in fact, when we hear of it, the Jewish, and perhaps, though not certainly, the early Celtic, Hades. But this was a very limited belief among Greeks at any time. Perhaps it represented one strain, accepted by some Greeks for a short time. Probably the Homeric Hades always remained a background of thought; but it was not the whole.

Homer actually attenuates the general pagan doctrine of survival as spirits in an underworld. He goes particularly far, for to him the spirits are normally cut off, do not return, and do not receive offerings after the time of their funeral. If the dead are confined powerless in a Hades, neglect of them is perhaps logical, but it is an exception to the usual pagan practice. The one important exception to Homer's exceptional assumption is the burial of Patroclus (pp. 47–8 above). Here there are offerings, and other details belonging to the opposite theory and compatible with later Greek practice, in which offerings were regularly made to the dead. It is supposed that Homer broke away from earlier habits of thought, returning to them significantly this once, but that the earlier habits continued as before for many centuries after Homer.

Homer's general scheme could be based on the appearances of ghosts and the plain fact that the dead are put under the ground and can be presumed to stay there. Their attributes in such passages, in Greece and elsewhere, how they cluster, have little sense, twitter in a thin voice, and flit, may be transferences from other creatures, bats perhaps, or other species seen to live in places believed to house spirits of the dead. The spirits are sometimes thought to come up through holes in the ground. There is a story of Africans in despair because a dam was to be built at exactly the spot where the spirits of their dead fellow-tribesmen regularly came out of the ground. Conversely, it has just been reported that some Tibetans protest against any deep mines being sunk in their territory, for fear that the spirits of their dead might be enabled to return. Either attitude may be adopted, according to the good or bad impression made on survivors by the behaviour of the departed.

Pre-civilised societies would never think of regarding the spirits as unreal. It has been stated that some Africans were holding a meeting of their tribal council. At the end of the meeting, many members walked off home. The others just vanished. The tribesmen, and indeed a European who was present, had no doubt that the visitors were dead ancestors, normally enough contributing good advice to their descendants.[7] It has also been reported that in Borneo deceased members of each family walk in and out of their home every day, advising on the upbringing of children and so forth, sometimes even too often and too insistently for the patience of the earthly family.[8] It is said that Jomo Kenyatta explicitly opposes Christianity as unsuitable for Africa, and means to return to 'ancestral spiritualism'. He is clearly a long way from Homer.[9]

The twittering, tenuous ghosts observed, or supposedly observed, by some are very different from certain other manifestations. The reason which is sometimes suggested in such comparisons is that the spirit-world is, like our earthly world, a big and various place containing many and various inhabitants.

Homer or his informants seem to have met the less vigorous, less blessed spirits. Perhaps some people have gone to, or heard about, the wrong part of the spirit-world. It is often, and authoritatively, said that living people, if they get into contact with spirits, meet spirits morally akin to themselves, since like attracts like. If so, the Egyptians deserve much credit, and the Sumerians and early Homeric Greeks distinctly less. We remember that at Gilgamesh's séance Enkidu returned, and gave a depressing account of his new home. What these particular ancients, or some of them, overlooked was the possibility of progress. Spirits might at first live weakly in a dim world, but go on and up to better conditions after. Many have thought, and many still think, that this regularly happens, even to great sinners. Homer should have expected even Tityos to be released one day.[10] However, at least he recognises a heavenly life for some.

The Homeric system leaves a certain gap, in that helpful spirits ought surely to be returning to help their earthly friends and relatives. This gap is perfectly filled by the mysterious Hesiod of Ascra in Boeotia, the didactic instructor-poet who was probably Homer's later contemporary and was thought to have written *The Works and Days, The Birth of the Gods*, and other poems. In the first of these occurs the passage for which he is most famous, the account of the Ages of Man, the Golden, the Silver, the Bronze, the Heroic, and the Iron Ages. Hesiod is living in the Age of Iron, and wishes he were not. It is a tale of progressive decay.

But what he has to say of the after-life of the men of the Golden Age is one of the most important statements on eschatology to be found anywhere outside the Bible. The Golden Men lived on earth, having free intercourse with the Gods.

They died; and became good and helpful spirits, wandering over the earth, observing righteous and unrighteous actions, and helping those who are good (*Works and Days*, 121-6).[11] The statement is succinct indeed. It is hard to think of a parallel. But Plato (*c.* 429-347 B.C.) at least seems to agree when in the *Phaedrus* (230 C and 258 E—259 C; cf. 262 D) he pictures— with characteristic humour—the dead, in the form of cicadas, sitting in a tree and taking notes of what people, unaware that they are being noticed, are doing. Hesiod's doctrine cannot be traced back to any original. It is true that the doctrine of the Ages of Man has Eastern prototypes, in the myth in which dethroned High Gods, forecasting the Greek Uranus and Cronos, lived, imprisoned, in a golden land below the earth.[12] But for us the conceptions of guardian angels, once good men on earth, and of recording angels too, conceptions alike precious and held today by many to be literally true, begin with Hesiod.

The whole doctrine of Hesiod's Five Ages is sophisticated and very old in origin. Its history in Asia goes back to a remote past. But the statement about the spirits of the good is in no way wrongly elaborated. It is clearly the direct experience of good men to whom has been revealed the true activity of spirits in harmony with them. Like has attracted like.

For Hesiod, the spirits of at least some of the dead associate, perceived or unperceived, with the living. They travel freely above ground. They are not confined to their tombs, some world below the earth, or any western land or Isles of the Blest. They exist, normally no doubt invisible, in the air with the living. This is probably the truth, so far as it goes. Hesiod has accepted an apparent impossibility, and chosen it well.

Homer differs greatly from Hesiod. But Homer himself accepts the invisibility of gods. His gods are part of his poetry. They are not part of a creed. Readers can if they like, and indeed it is easier, treat them as imaginative creations. Homer was himself not certainly believing in invisibility as literally as Hesiod seems to believe in it. One gives us elaborated poetry; the other folklore.

Unlike Hesiod, Homer normally assumes that the dead and the living have no contact with each other. For Homer, if a supernatural or other-worldly being helps, hinders or otherwise affects a living man, it will be a deity, not the spirit of a dead man. But there is more to say. Homer's gods are sometimes visible and sometimes invisible to mortals. Sometimes they are concealed in a mist and they can conceal a mortal in a mist. When he lets a god withdraw the veil from a mortal's eyes ('I have taken the mist from your eyes', Athena to Diomedes, *Iliad* v, 127), or lets him assume or bestow a cloud of concealment (*Iliad* XVII, 551; *Odyssey* VII, 40–2; cf. p. 137 below), Homer may, as Professor T. J. Haarhoff has suggested, be reflecting some relation to what is known as 'the psychic mist' (i.e. a mist accompanying certain types of phenomena). Hesiod called his good spirits '*daimones*'. The word '*daimon*' usually means a spirit. Rohde observes that Homer uses it freely as a synonym of the word for god, '*theos*'.[13] Homer's gods often behave like good spirits or guardian angels.[14] Individual deities aid and protect human individuals and groups. Hera acts for the Greeks in general, Apollo for the Trojans, and so on. Thetis takes care of her son Achilles and Athena of Diomedes and Odysseus. Thanks to Homer's pattern of belief, and also to our patterns of belief, all this seems to be fancy and poetry and perhaps theology. It may be no more than that; but it is hard to read the penetrating French Hellenist, Professor Fernand Robert, in the relevant part of his book on Homer,[15] without seeing in the intervention of Homeric deities a representation of general human experience, when some external but invisible agency seems to intervene with a stroke of good or bad luck. Often the deity just puts a thought into the mind of a hero.[16] Looked at in this way, the Homeric world becomes instinct with gods and spirits, or gods or spirits, through and through. He illustrates the Heraclitean or perhaps rather the Stoic assertion that the world is full of gods, an assertion which in one form or another became almost an orthodoxy in later antiquity. Perhaps the sensitive mind of John Cowper Powys was not engaged in any very different topic when in his *Homer*

and the Aether ('The Aether Speaks', 24) he accorded chief ad-
miration to the vitality of all things in Homer's poetry.

A god to us is transcendent and exalted, and so often enough
he was to Greeks. But in Greek *theos* can be applied to many
quite different things. Good fortune or prosperity is 'a god'.
Even a drink of water can be called 'a god'. We are not so
very far from the usage of the backward peoples; the African
Masai apply their word for god, *ngai*, to any material things
which strike them as wonderful, such as the tents and other
equipment carried by European travellers. Modern learning,
right within special terms of reference, has drawn the line
very firmly between gods and other spirits, such as heroes;
but such a strong distinction can be deceptive. In late times the
Neoplatonists and others seem to use the word '*theos*' very
freely for visiting spirits who are certainly nowhere near Olympian rank, even though they may be themselves distinguished
from lower visitants such as angels.

Accordingly, Homer can be seen as representing through
his poetic imagery the influence of discarnate spirits on living
men which Hesiod stated directly. It is not impossible for a
mortal to be revered after death as a god; such is not the origin
of Homer's gods;[17] but at least there is a possible or even a
probable relation between the two poets in respect to this most
important truth. Homer had no need to emphasise contact between living men and departed spirits, since he was dealing with
the truth of intercourse between the two worlds when he pictured his divine interventions; and it is surely fair to soften
down the distinction usually drawn between Hesiod's spirits of
the good, who guide and guard men still on earth, and Homer's
Olympians who guide and guard their favourite heroes. We
have only to be impressed by the volume and intensity of artistic
and theological activity which eventually created the glittering
and sharply contoured Olympian Family.

5 Tombs Shrines Heroes

Both Homer and Hesiod present word-pictures of a happy land beyond death. So do later Greek writers. These word-pictures are similar to each other. The happy land has good weather, and the earth freely gives its produce, without the necessity of work. All is happiness and righteousness. This topic became a traditional motive, and writer after writer develops it, often with literary skill and imagination. Dr. Helena da Rocha-Pereira has collected and discussed these word-pictures in writers from Homer to Plato.[1] Some refer to a heaven, on Olympus or in Isles of the Blest or elsewhere, to which some human beings go after their life on earth. Some, on the other hand, give an imaginative impression of a place on earth, some fancied utopia or a place in fairyland,

It is possible to think that these conceptions began because someone in Hesiod's position, impressed by the hardship of his own life on a poor farm, constructed an entirely opposite conception, and described an ideal life as different as possible from the real life familiar to him, and that other writers took up the conception and applied it as their purposes required. No doubt one of the early applications was to some Golden Age in the past, which had been imagined long before Greek times and has parallels elsewhere. But the Egyptian idea of a heaven is also much earlier than Greek times, and the first application of ideal conditions of life to a land of the dead may have been made by Greeks long before Homer and Hesiod. In any case it is necessary to distinguish three things, the idea itself which is obvious enough, its literary development and its application. However it started, and whatever words were used for it, and whatever uses were made of it, it remains possible that when it was applied to some other-worldly heaven, someone may have thought the application true to fact, and may even have thought so with good reason.

On the whole the differing and rather incompatible beliefs about the dead held by the Greeks belong to classes of belief widely held in other parts of the world at various times and are traceable to direct experience of ghosts. Neither in Greece nor elsewhere is a critical interpretation of the evidence for beliefs always noticeable. But there must always be at least a little interpretation, explicit or implicit, when beliefs are expressed and communicated, even in folklore. Some inferences are quickly made, for example the inference that the dead, having entered the earth at burial, continue to exist under the surface, and, since there are very many of them, must have some space there, so that some kind of Hades becomes a necessity of thought. It is not, however, obvious to everyone that the ghost must be where the body is. Nevertheless people have often, and perhaps at first always, found it hard to imagine these two parts of a man, separately. The ghost looks like the body. Its independence of the body, though understood by some people thousands of years ago, might not have been at all easily understood by others. Even the Egyptians, who like other peoples worked out an elaborate description of the parts which combine to make a human personality, retained their belief in a spatial underworld, while also having a strong belief in a heaven, there or elsewhere.

The question is whether the belief in heaven and the happy conditions there can possibly be based on direct evidence and so included in folklore, not fanciful idealism. It is most probable that it is. Homer took a depressing version, but a very simple one, and also the most tragic, and the one most in place for his poetry. The other side of the picture is far from simple, but it has a certain unity.

The dead lived under the earth or in a far world, not below

the earth but on the surface, like the living. This is myth. It is an expression and an amplification of experience. The experience itself was of ghosts, or supposed ghosts (but I will leave 'supposed' to be understood—no one denies that some people have supposed that they saw ghosts), and experience belongs to living people on earth. Reacting to it, these living people—outside Homer—sacrificed to the dead at their tombs, perhaps at an annual All Souls' Day, perhaps on the anniversary of the death, or perhaps on some special occasion, as in Aeschylus' *Choephori* (see below). In known examples of Greek tombs there is a pipe leading from the top down to the place where the remains of the dead had been laid so that drink offerings could be poured straight in, to reach the physical body, as last seen. After decomposition drink could hardly revive the body. It must have been meant to revive the spirit, conceived as being where the body was or had been. From the tomb came spirits, such as the spirit of Darius in Aeschylus' *Persae*, who appeared as a ghost to the living.

There was a strict distinction between offerings to the dead and offerings to the gods. The altars were different. A god had an altar, a *bōmos*; the dead had a hearth, *eschara*. A god had a burnt sacrifice, roast meat. The normal custom was for a dead man to have uncooked offerings, meal, honey, and milk. The words for sacrifice were different, to a god *thyein*, and to a dead person *enagizein*. Normally, the dead had a tomb but not an altar. In Aeschylus' *Choephori* (106) the Chorus says 'We reverence your father's tomb, as if it was an altar', shewing the distinction. There was perhaps a 'hearth' of some kind. There were indeed two sorts of dead, or rather living dead, ordinary people, and heroes. A hero, or heroine, was a dead man or woman who was specially respected for great and useful, or dangerous, qualities, and honoured with prayers or offerings, at a shrine, *herōon*, not a temple, *hieron*, with a hearth, *eschara*, not an altar, *bōmos*. So much attention was paid to the ordinary, and to the heroic, dead, that it proves that the Greeks, except perhaps for the limited group, wherever it was, who gave Homer his ideas on the subject, assumed that the dead continued

to live, to have feelings, and to be able to act—some very effectively. According to Herodotus (VI, 61), Helen at Therapne could
make an ugly baby beautiful if it were taken to her shrine and
the right prayers were said; though this 'Helen' may have been
more goddess than heroine.[2] For heroes, the tomb remained
important. Spirits, like the Egyptian king's 'soul bird' returning
to his tomb chamber, could come back to it, or mainly stayed
in or near it. But they certainly travelled about freely, and might
turn up far away. A great deal has always depended on the immense mobility of spirits, a mobility which has always seemed
mysterious and inexplicable—till now, when anyone, holding
these beliefs and wanting a suitable hypothesis, can get one
from the conceptions of modern physics (p. 96 below).

In general, Greek 'heroes' in the technical sense seem to us
much less important than they seemed to the Greeks themselves.
Hero-shrines were everywhere. Heroes and heroines were
men and women who had been promoted at death to a particular
semi-divine status, a power to help or to harm people living on
the earth. They are not unlike saints, marabouts, and 'worthies'.
Indeed, there is an attractive theory of J. D. Unwin that they
have a regular place in the development of all normal human
societies, on the way from what he terms a 'zoistic' through a
'manistic' (for *manes* see p. 108 below) to a 'deistic' stage, in
which the object of belief is always concurrent with a corresponding sexual code: as the code becomes stricter, the objects
of tendance or worship become more individualised, fewer, and
more majestic. In the beginning the dead were tended in an
undifferentiated mass. At or near the end of the process is a
monotheism concurrent with monogamy.[3] The ancient Greeks
had in their Hades a reminiscence of some manistic condition.
Their zoistic stage is more emphatically remembered, for their
hero-cult was continuous, important and widespread. Their
deistic stage overlapped it. They reached a certain occasional
monotheism. It is hard not to call Plato a monotheist. The more
emphatic Greek monotheisms must acknowledge Iranian or
Hebrew influence.

The heroes of cult have the same names as the heroes of epic. But otherwise they are very different. In epic, heroes are human but gifted and powerful, and meanwhile the dead have no contact with the living. In cult, heroes may be much less human; they may be little more than a name, or even seem more animal than human. But they are active and powerful, and needed propitiation as much as, or more than, gods, who were normally more aloof. New heroes were still being canonised late in the fifth century B.C.

Heroes could do good, like Helen at Therapne. Several appearances of heroes are recorded. Theseus appeared, leading the Athenians and smiting the Persians, at Marathon (Plutarch, *Life of Theseus*, 35). In our own time there was the belief in the Angels of Mons. They may have been seen[4]; probably enough Theseus was too. Some heroes gave oracles, especially Amphiaraus and Trophonius.[5] Their names contrast. 'Amphiaraus' is a suitable name for a living man such as the mythical prince to whom it belongs. 'Trophonius' is more functional; it seems to mean something like 'Feeder' or 'Fructifier'. Some Greeks were aware of strong influences which could be effective for good, and reasonably attributed them to spirits, no doubt seen by some, though whether the spirits were rightly identified with men who had lived on earth must often, if not most often, have been obscure. Nor was it necessary to know what kind of life the spirit or hero lived in order to propitiate him. Heroes are a proof that many Greeks believed in an active after-life for some, but not an indication to shew what they thought this after-life to be like. Achilles, feared as a furious *daimon* dangerous to seafarers, was thought to live above ground, haunting the 'White Island' on the Black Sea (e.g. Pausanias, III, XIX, 13). Trophonius lived in his cave: a proper and logical home for many heroes. But already at the end of the sixth century B.C. Achilles and Diomedes are placed in the Isles of the Blest in the Drinking Song,[6] and Harmodius and Aristogeiton the tyrannicides have joined them there (p. 73 below). The Isles of the Blest became an admittedly suitable home for heroes and a suitable location of the heaven, earthly heaven, or summer-land of the poetic word-pictures. But the whole conception could be treated as mere poetry, and increasingly was, at least for a time. It was easy to think that no heaven existed except perhaps for gods. It was also easy to be much less sure that heroes did not exist, and affect human life. Worse inconsistencies than that are common enough.

As usual, direct experience was there but readily faded in the obscurity of apparent incompatibilities. In the Eleventh *Odyssey* Heracles' ghost is in Hades but he is also with the Immortals (*Odyssey* XI, 601–4). This distinction is paralleled in other places (see p. 50 and note 6). There are separable parts of the person-ality, and they can be in different places at once. So, as we shall see (p. 73), Hermotimus of Clazomenae divided himself. But humanity, if used to reasoning, does not like to believe the apparently impossible. It often prefers to believe something that really is impossible, and call it miraculous. There are and usually have been plenty of difficulties. If ghosts exist, they ought not to be so often invisible; other beings are not. If they are moving about on the earth it is strange that they are also in their graves, and so on. But late in the classical Greek period something came in to help. Eastern thought about the air and the stars gradually accustomed Greeks to think that beings might live invisibly in space, even high up in it. Even heaven and hell are presently located in the air. The supreme attainment is very high, with gods near or on the sun. Or the moon is the lower sphere of the hereafter, the sun the higher, and the space be-tween intermediate—a rudimentary heaven, hell and purgatory.

There are two main strains of belief. The dead lived in an underground Hades, or elsewhere, and no more was heard of them. Alternatively, the dead survived and were active and very mobile. Of these two beliefs, the second is much the more important. But it is all as seen from the point of view of those still living the earthly life. There is also the point of view of the dead themselves—and not only as attributed by Homer to Patroclus in *Iliad* XXII, and to Achilles in *Odyssey* XI.

To find this out there were, and are, two important methods, the same as indicated in the *Odyssey*. We can go to the dead or they can come to us. In ancient Egypt not only was contact with the world, and spirits, of the dead regularly sought and practised (p. 33 above, note 2); the dead man was also invited to visit and make merry with his companions on earth:

Let him drink the water of the wells,
may he have sexual delights.
And the great company that is in the Field says—
Let him sing and dance and put on garlands,
allow him to play draughts with those upon earth
and may his voice be heard although he is not seen,
let him return to his house and call his mates together for ever and a day.
Then will that Spirit say:
    'I have come here to summon my boon companions'.[7]

There is a vivid sense of what might be called 'companionship'.

These beliefs have considerable continuity, if not universality. Tribal societies have stories—E. B. Tylor recounted some[8]—of living people who have visited the land of the dead and returned, as Odysseus, Aeneas, and Dante did, in the stories about them. In Greek myth Theseus and Heracles went and returned. In the beginning this very journey is the subject of the Babylonian epic *Gilgamesh*. At about the time when Homer seems to have lived, and during the next two centuries or so, between about 700 and 500 B.C., the Greek world took an interest in such abnormalities. Herodotus has tales of Aristeas of Proconnesus and Abaris the Hyperborean (see p. 73 and note 7, below), who had mysterious powers of mobility; and these tales may have been confused accounts of what is today known as 'astral travel'. The men concerned are historical characters, but obscure. What exactly they did or said is hardly certain. But the stories become more convincing when they are aligned with other stories, other reported or even certainly known occurrences, with which they can, and should, be classified. Among these examples are accounts left by such early Greek philosophers as Parmenides (born *c.* 515 B.C.) and Empedocles (*c.* 493–*c.* 433 B.C.), who report their experiences of the spiritual world behind the phenomena of earth.[9]

If in ancient Egypt 'Osiris', symbolising the dead, came back to his friends, he may very well, in modern terms, have appeared to them, or to those among them who had second-sight, as a ghost or a materialised spirit. If they went to see him, or if anyone else, such as Odysseus, ever made such a journey, there is again a modern term for this other very old occurrence. These visitors fell into a trance, and their souls or spirits went on astral travel. That the soul is detachable from the body and can travel far alone is a familiar pre-civilised belief, and a basis for legends and folklore. True or false, it is, under the name of astral travel, a familiar belief today. There are many people who sincerely believe that they have travelled in sleep; I do myself. We should clearly classify all the visitors to the other world in the same category as astral travellers. Meanwhile, information about the other world is freely communicated by spirits of the dead to clairvoyants. Several of their descriptions have been printed during the last few years. They fit the Greek descriptions of a heaven very well. Probability is strongly on the side of the view that some Greeks knew this brighter aspect of the other world by direct experience of one kind or another no less than they knew the ghosts. Even if it were all lies, it would still come under the same classification. We shall see this even more clearly when we come to discuss Plato and Aristotle.

It will now be hard to deny that the ancient Greeks, or many of them, thought that they had some knowledge of the other world through direct experience, either by second-sight or by astral travel during trance, the wanderings of 'detachable souls'. The knowledge was expressed with different degrees and kinds of mythologisation. The descent to Hades was most normal, at least in early times. Indeed, it goes back to ancient Egypt and the Asiatic myth of the Goddess Ishtar's descent to the world below. But at least someone had always had a direct experience, or was thought to have had.

Early Greeks seem to have agreed with many other peoples in various places in their faith in social distinctions. Most of the dead go to Hades. A few, royal or partly divine, go to a heaven. In *Gilgamesh*, divine favour allows the voyager to pass to the beyond. Vergil is the first epic poet to add moral merit as a qualification. In these matters it is hard always to remember the enormous effect of differences in ethical philosophy. Even in the standard Greek mythology, that is, mythology as it is without poetic moralisation, it has been observed that no Greek hero has credit for any moral qualities. Early peoples, conscious of dangers, taboos, and the complicated actions on which good luck depends, hardly look at things morally. Many are good men, but they hardly see themselves in such a light. To be royal or aristocratic is to be good; even the historic Greeks used the word for 'good', *esthlos*, equally to mean 'aristocratic'. Therefore social position was at first for those, as for many others, the qualification for a life in a heaven.

E

6 Prophecy Oracles

From about the time of Homer and Hesiod or soon after there was a quick development in Greece mainly because there was a period of great psychic sensitivity. Hesiod's beautiful expression of a great truth concerning the spirits of good men is hard to parallel at all exactly, but there is a great departure from Homer's more theological world-view. For Homer the superhuman or supernatural is normally the divine. Prophecy in particular is emphatically subject to Olympian gods, Apollo, or Zeus. It is the priest who counts, not some less authoritative and perhaps irresponsible clairvoyant. But in the practical Greek world outside Homer the gifts of the spirit were not always so easily canalised. They were indeed manifested multifariously. Much is recorded concerning what went on. But it is not always clear how to interpret the record.

Much of what we are told comes under two favourite conceptions, *mantikē*, 'prophecy', and *catharsis*, 'purification'. Neither must necessarily be taken to have anything to do with an after-life. That they might have is strongly, if indirectly, suggested by the views of Professor E. R. Dodds,[1] who points out that *mantikē* should be taken to cover many paranormal phenomena, and Erwin Rohde,[2] who shews that *catharsis* must often mean purification by the ejection of a possessing or obsessing spirit. There was of course necromancy, prophecy specifically elicited by consultation of the dead at oracles of the dead, *necyomanteia*, of which there were many; and there is a very famous story in Herodotus (v, 92) about one of them, on the river Acheron in Epirus, where Periander of Corinth (ruled *c.* 625–585 B.C.) asked a question of his dead wife, and received a satisfactory answer. Such a death oracle and such a séance are no doubt remembered in the eleventh *Odyssey*, where, in contrast to the normal Homeric assumption, Odysseus consulted the spirits of his mother Anticleia and of Teiresias.

At a *necyomanteion* prophecy may well have come from the dead, surviving in an after-life. Other prophecy might, of course, have various different origins. It might be sham, just guess-work, or even based on some encyclopaedic knowledge such has been imputed, in the old too exclusive theory, to the Delphic priesthood. Prophecy might even, though we should hardly believe this, come from Apollo himself; or from some entirely obscure intuitive faculty in the prophet or prophetess. Clearly the Delphic Oracle itself often, if not always, operated as a *necyomanteion*. In the historical period it was owned by Apollo, who claimed through his priests the responsibility for the predictions and advice given. But he was by no means the first occupant of the shrine, or the first oracular being to have claimed the authorship of the prophecy there.

Apollo's most famous prophetesses were at Delphi. Now it is widely believed on good evidence that many, if not all, of the Delphic prophetesses were in fact mediums.[3] They were controlled by spirits, and the voices of these spirits spoke through them. Modern authorities who are not themselves spiritualists, believe this. There is, especially, the testimony of Plutarch (*c.* A.D. 46—after 120): a prophetess who had been forced to submit to trance before she was ready spoke under inspiration in a harsh voice[4] and soon after died of the shock (Plutarch, *De Defectu Oraculorum*, 438 A–C; cf. Lucan, *Pharsalia* v, 161 ff.) This is appropriate to a medium, and a medium only.[5]

Apollo had taken Delphi away from earlier possessors. The first, says Aeschylus in the *Eumenides*, had been 'Earth, primal prophetess'. Apollo arrogated prophecy to himself. It was not to be capricious, but compressed within the Olympian religion. Calchas, says Homer, was a good prophet. He guided the Greek ships to Troy by means of his prophetic skill 'which Phoebus Apollo had given to him' (*Iliad* I, 69–72); it has been suggested that the last words may be an addition, to sustain Apollo's claim.

In Roman times Cicero (p. 122 below) carefully distinguished between scientific prophecy, done by knowledge of the rules, 'art', *ars*, and inspired, 'mad', prophecy, *furor*. The difference was later admitted, but little clear conception of control by a spirit occurs at any early date. A great deal of the phenomena would have been more easily understood in antiquity if sufficient notice had been accorded to the theory, if it is no more than a theory, of control. This attention is now due. Possession, that is permanent occupation of a living human body by 'a discarnate entity', was widely recognised. In the early centuries A.D. things became clearer. But before that much was conceded to the mysterious abilities of 'prophets', *manteis*, who 'purified' many. Apparently today they would be called clairvoyants and mediums, with the gifts of prediction and spiritual healing, who were able to perform exorcisms—'casting out evil spirits'.

During their earlier centuries the Greeks had little easy, happy intercourse with the spirits as, for example, did the Getae (p. 77 below). Their relations with them were framed in rituals, perhaps lightly framed, not rigidly as they were to be among the Romans. More or less behind the scenes there was wizardry. Wizards intimidated spirits of the dead and compelled them to fulfil their own normally evil purposes. This is how they are understood later, in the earliest Christian centuries, as Apollonius of Tyana, a philosophising mystic of the first century A.D. (pp. 145–7 below), and Eusebius (A.D. 260–340), criticising him, reveal. Apollonius was always anxious not to be thought a wizard, but a 'philosopher'; which meant, among other things, a spiritualist with good intentions (p. 154 below). Among the less presentable rites, with which wizards, *goëtes*, could be concerned, was necromancy: prophecy by means of a dead body. Much of this went on in many places. It is not, or at least should not be taken to mean, consultation of a dis-

embodied spirit. The plan was to revive a corpse, and converse
with it. (Such a performance is fully described by Lucan (A.D.
39–65) in the Sixth Book of the *Pharsalia*. Pompey visits an
expert witch, who revives the body of a soldier killed a few
days before in the battle.)

This unpleasant practice is not so familiar now. If a spirit is
encountered, the spirit is without his old material body, and
appears in some kind of astral or etheric form unless he material-
ises; that is, appears in a new body, which looks like his old one
but is in fact newly built of ectoplasm. St. Paul in particular
emphasises the spiritual body: he is strongly opposed to the other
belief, that the material body is to persist and will rise at the
Resurrection (p. 151 below). Now the earlier Greeks were well
aware of disembodied spirits, light as air. Surely when in Herodotus (p. 66 above) a man talked to his dead wife, we are meant
to think that he talked to her spirit, not her revivified corpse.
Yet the word for a place where spirits could be met and invited to
talk was *nekyomanteion*, a 'corpse-oracle', not a 'spirit-oracle'.
It is tempting to think that the Greeks encountered spirits usually
as we do, but extended the names of corpse-prophecy and corpse-
oracle, *nekyomanteia* and *nekyomanteion*, to cover what we should
regard as normal spirit-return. Why this happened, if it did, is
obscure. The reason may be connected with some not entirely
candid policy among the managers of the oracles. A picture of a
revived body may have impressed visitants. Or possibly dead
bodies were not revived, which so far as I know may be impossible, but materialised spirits were, as sometimes now, encountered, and regarded as revived corpses. This is not absurd.
The ancients had no theory of materialisation, at least in the
earlier periods. Not knowing that the materialised form was a
new creation, they would almost have had to regard it as a
corpse, the appearance being the same, and no harm done. At
any rate, here is a point where ancient and modern spiritualism
differ, as they seldom do. Either corpse-revival was ancient and
not modern, or the ancients were deceived for lack of understanding of the psychic fact of materialisation. If the first, it is

very strange. If the second, it is gratifying to think that some progress has been made in psychic science. Often enough it is tempting to think that not much has.

As science broke off from philosophy, so the branches of psychic science broke off from a Greek blanket conception, the conception of prophecy, *manteia*, by prophets, *manteis*. Prophecy covered any surprising or unusual knowledge; it covered healing and, especially, exorcism; a prophet might even affect the weather, as Empedocles, and indeed Elijah himself, are said to have done. Calchas the prophet guided the Greek ships to Troy. The general ability of a prophet covered ordinary practical and theoretical knowledge, but it also included all the branches of the paranormal. Accordingly, the Greek use of the words for prophet and prophesy can be misleading to us. They conceal interesting facts which have to be elicited by analysis.

Certainly the Greeks had a great, and convinced, belief in prophecy and the inspiration which belonged to it. Prophets could be, ought to be, natural, gifted. But they were often thought to be directed, or possessed, by Apollo. There was an adjective *Phoebolamptos*, 'seized by Apollo', which denoted 'inspired', that is, inspired to prophesy. They had other words: one is *ecstaticos*, 'standing outside', that is, having part of the self, the soul or mind or spirit, outside the body, presumably now in some place where it is close to truth, so that the only conception which would fit the word, according to our knowledge and notions, would be astral projection, a correspondence probable enough. There is a third adjective, equally intriguing. It is *entheos*, meaning 'with God inside', and it can hardly help meaning 'controlled by a god or spirit', since one of our most important facts is the ability of words such as *theos*, 'god', to mean any one of many gradations of dignity, from Zeus the highest God, or even God Himself, down through many lower gods and spirits as far as plain 'prosperity', which Aeschylus calls a god, and even a drink of water. Such semantic variety is probably normal among less advanced cultures (p. 56 above).

All this needs to be noticed. A narrow, modern interpretation of pagan words for 'god' can be disastrously misleading.

The ordinary information concerning Greek prophecy and prophets plainly suggests that some outside intelligence was thought to take over. Even at Delphi the prophetesses, or at least many of them, are now authoritatively thought to have been mediums. One story, already told here, is specially evocative—how a priestess died after being unnaturally forced into trance. This sad event suggests some variety of spirit-control (p. 67 above, note 4). If those present had known what we know it would not have been allowed to happen. But an accident, or malice, is possible.

Herodotus (I, 47) tells us that King Croesus sent messengers from Sardis to various oracles to enquire what he was doing on the hundredth day after they left the city. This was a test, and it worked. Only Delphi prophesied correctly, saying that he had cut up a tortoise and lamb and boiled them in a cauldron with a bronze lid on it. A favourite test in antiquity was to send a sealed letter to see if it could be read unopened. Macrobius (*Saturnalia* I, 23, 14 f.) describes how the Emperor Trajan sent a sealed set of blank tablets to the oracle of Jupiter Heliopolitanus at Baalbek. The tablets were returned with the seal unbroken. A second letter contained the god's answer: when broken open it too contained a blank sheet. Sometimes, no doubt, such tests were met by cheating, but certainly not always, any more than at present.

The Delphic prophetesses are not unlike other inspired women of the early period of Greek history, the sibyls. They are distinguished from them; but at least one sibyl had once occupied the Delphic tripod. Sibyls are always interesting. They occur on the fringe of the Greek world. They go into trances with signs of great emotion, hair streaming, mouth foaming. Nowadays mediums usually slip quietly into a trance, but not always. However in Asia mediums are still expected to shew signs of disturbance such as the sibyls shewed. They were undoubtedly mediums, and that is all the more certain because they were some-

times thought to be not only prophetesses, but also guardians at
the gate of the world of the dead.

Cassandra, at least once called a sibyl,[6] the Trojan princess
loved and deserted by Apollo, who gave her the gift of prophecy
but then, because she had resisted his love, ordained that her
prophecy should never be believed, does not seem to have
been 'controlled' by a spirit. In the *Agamemnon* of Aeschylus,
she seems to read off the House's bloodstained past from the
scene before her, seeing the palace stained with blood. This
is today called 'psychometry', the act of reading off the history
and human associations of objects touched by the psychometrist.
She also foresees the immediate future, Agamemnon's murder
and her own. Here she is apparently being controlled by Apollo
himself, as the Cumaean Sibyl in the Sixth Book of Vergil's
Aeneid is explicitly controlled by Apollo after she is entranced
(*Aeneid* VI, 45–51; 77–82).

If the human dead came back as spirits they could tell their
friends, still on earth, what their life in the other world was like.
That this could happen is suggested by an account of an experiment in which a boy's soul, after being astrally projected by use
of a mysterious 'rod', came back and 'reported every detail'
(p. 94 below). In the third and fourth centuries A.D. there was
plenty of exact knowledge. Human, besides other, spirits were
known to control mediums, and there are technical terms for
what happens: for instance, a medium is a 'receiver', *docheus*.

This short sketch of the evidence ought to be enough. There
should be no reasonable doubt that in early times Greeks were
(supposedly at least) getting information about the other world
by spirit communication through prophet-mediums. Often if
not always when we hear of a corpse-oracle we ought to be
hearing of this. What this information was is not said. But
human beings have imagined an earthly paradise very much
like the best that the earth can furnish, as when in the time of
the Persian Hassan-i-Sabbah a beautiful garden was provided
to convince chosen victims that here was a foretaste of Heaven,
so that thay should wish to die.

At the end of the sixth century Harmodius and Aristogeiton liberated Athens from tyranny. In The Drinking Song (p. 61 above) we have: 'I will carry my sword in a bough of myrtle, like Harmodius and Aristogeiton, who killed the tyrant, and gave Athens freedom under law. Dearest Harmodius, you are not dead, oh no, for they say that you are in the Isles of the Blest, where is Achilles the fleet-footed and the noble Diomedes, son of Tydeus'. The thought comes quite naturally.

At this early historical period, 700 to 500 B.C., there was a general outbreak of peculiar powers in, perhaps in and near, Greece. There are, as we have seen, stories of 'detachable souls' or 'astral travel'.[7] Aristeas of Proconnesus and Abaris the Hyperborean are said to have disappeared, to have been seen in a distant place, and to have come back to tell their experiences (Herodotus IV, 13–16 and 36). Whether these journeys were physical or purely psychic is not clear. Hermotimus of Clazomenae was credited with having stayed away for years, and with having seen and reported occurrences which happened far from the place where his entranced body still lay; returning to give an account of his astral travels (Apollonius, *Historiae mirabiles* 3). Epimenides of Crete (sixth century B.C.) travelled similarly. He was also believed to have conversed with gods during an extended sleep. Both Hermotimus and Epimenides returned from their astral travels enriched with an other-worldly wisdom. Epimenides was famous for his prophecy and his 'purifications'. In prophecy he specialised in revealing the present and the past rather than the future. Such prophecy is sometimes easy to test. It happens, of course, today, often by a direct sensitivity to objects in what is called 'psychometry'. The stories look legendary and are hard to believe if we do not admit that psychic powers exist and paranormal occurrences happen. If we do, the stories, even though here and there apparently exaggerated, become quickly intelligible, and reveal a new and extremely important strain in history.

7   *Mystery Religions*

All these ancient Greek notions were part of a general belief based on the experience of individuals. People listened to poets, and heard the versions of those who were thought to have penetrated the veil. Meanwhile, with this background and out of this soil, there grew associations for the right religious behaviour towards the other world in view of the soul's believed destiny. A considerable knowledge—some would say a supposed knowledge—existed. Some people decided to act carefully upon it.

It has been said that all religions are principally concerned with death.[1] It has also been observed that fertility cults and the worship or tendance of the dead always go together. Such generalisations are hard to prove but they may still be useful. They are a warning against the assumption that a rite, which appears to be intelligible as a fertility-rite, designed to secure the growth of animal and vegetable life, cannot therefore also be a death-rite, a form of attention given to dead parents and ancestors.

During this same period, several forms of personal and mystical religion either started or became prominent. Classical Greece had four very notable mystery religions, the Eleusinian Mysteries, Orphism, Pythagoreanism and the cult of Dionysus. A Mystery, *mysterion*, is concerned with secrets. To those who are initiated, secrets are opened, or revealed.

At the Eleusinian Mysteries, the Mysteries at Eleusis, a small town fourteen miles from Athens to the west, the culminating revelation is thought to have been an ear of corn. The myth belonging to the cult concerns the corn-goddess Demeter. But the life of dying mankind was concerned too. The Mysteries were universally revered. Initiates had to be not only ritually but to some extent also morally pure. The culminating ceremony was a sacred drama, perhaps enacting a marriage followed by the birth of a son, Brimos, from a mother, Brimo. Brimo was a goddess of death. The site belonged principally to Demeter, Persephone and Triptolemos. Of them Persephone was also a death goddess. But the first object seems to have been the productivity of the earth, especially in corn. This is no great incompatibility. Indeed it begins to appear, as Charles Autran said, that fertility-cults and death-cults not only tend to go together but are rather two sides of the same thing.[2] Independently A. Körte argued[3] that at Eleusis both the fertility of the earth and also the happiness after death of individual souls were sought. Certainly the ceremonies imparted to those present a feeling of bliss. They are not, however, known to have revealed anything about a future state. But, since they were kept very secret, that is no proof that they did not.

These Mysteries were certainly very old. The Hall of Initiation, called the *telesterion*, has been excavated. It goes back before 700 B.C.

Whether Orphism was as old is uncertain. Orphism was not an organised religion. There was no sort of Orphic church. But people known as Orphics believed and communicated a fluid but recognisable scheme of doctrine. It was said to have been founded by the mythical Orpheus, a famous lyre-player of Thrace who went down to Hades to bring back his dead wife Eurydice, but lost her again because he turned round to look at her on the way, and she vanished. Orphism had other myths, including one about the original creation of the world from a 'world egg'. Those who accepted Orphism joined together in local societies or lodges, and learnt the Orphic doctrines. They were directed how to live in moral purity, and what to do and say after death—reminding us of the Egyptian 'negative confession'. Again ritual, and to some extent moral, purity was required. The soul of an initiate would undergo reincarnations and in the end emerge as a pure spirit, living in a heaven among the stars. This belief among Greeks is sudden and new. Certainly their gods had been at home in the sky before. The Homeric Olympus itself is sometimes a sky-heaven and no longer a mountain. But hitherto the stars had not been in this context an urgent Greek interest. Eastern astrology reached Greece later. But Eastern astronomy or astral religion may have contributed to Orphic belief. The idea of reincarnation may also have come from the East; it is best known in India.

Orphism was to some extent a learned religion or faith. Poets and perhaps other thinkers worked out its implications. There were Orphic priests, and even magicians, who went round selling information, and spells also, a practice of which Plato disapproved (see p. 93 below). It is human to contaminate a life-giving idea or a great truth. Much Orphism was certainly respectable, especially in its earlier history.

Pythagoreanism was founded by Pythagoras, a historical character of about 570 to 500 B.C. who lived in Samos and then Croton, migrating from the coast of Asia Minor to the toe of Italy. Very little is known about him, but more about his followers and their interests and beliefs. Pythagoras kept a kind of advanced school, especially for music and mathematics, which was also a religious society, living according to strict beliefs, such as the belief in reincarnation and the transmigration of souls, and in ascetic practices. Towards the end of the pagan era Orphism and Pythagoreanism tended to coalesce, and turn into the notable system known as Neopythagoreanism.

The fourth mystery religion was the religion of Dionysus, who came also to be called Bacchus.[4] Dionysus was a strange god, perhaps primarily a god of moist vegetation such as fruit and the wine which came from it, whereas Demeter was Goddess of Corn, the dry crop. Dionysus was worshipped from an early date. Homer refers to him four times (*Iliad* VI, 132, 135 and XIV, 325; *Odyssey* XI, 325 and XXIV, 74). And his name is read by some on one of the Pylian Tablets in Linear B Mycenaean script, dated about 1220 B.C. Dionysus was a God of Ecstasy, whether due to wine or not. He freed his worshippers from restraints and inhibitions, so that they ran madly over the mountains, killing animals and eating them raw. The information about Dionysus is enormous, and much of it confirms his worship as a fertility-cult, but not only that. Dionysus was called 'lord of souls'.[5] He was said in antiquity to have come to Greece from abroad, some tracing him to Asia and some to Thrace. Probably enough his cult only became highly popular after 700 B.C. He may even have been introduced about this time from Thrace. In Thrace there was certainly among the Getae a strong cult of the dead centred on the Dionysian god Zalmoxis. The Getae were remarkable for their psychic sensitivity. Like the Bornese Bushmen, and some of the ancient Egyptians, they were in close and frequent contact with their dead relatives and friends, and enjoyed converse with them, in such a situation as is implied by Hesiod's record of the Golden Age, when men freely conversed with gods, and by other reports from other lands. These Getae lamented at a birth and rejoiced at a death, firmly believing that their lives would be far happier after death than before. They tended to asceticism, and some lived in strict celibacy, which probably helped their psychic power.[6] Lucan's description of Celts in the time of Nero (A.D. 54–68) closely agrees (*Pharsalia* I, 452–62): they are primarily concerned with the after-life.

Dionysus may well have occasioned at least some impression of such a style of living when his cult first came to Greece. He had many attributes and, as the cult spread and developed, the orgiastic side of it won especial attention. In Thrace he was a god of the dead, or rather of the living in the world beyond. He was always and everywhere a god of life and vitality. His similarity to Osiris in Egypt, which Herodotus (II, 42, 144, 156) stresses, makes him easier to understand. Both gods died and rose again. Both were gods of the living dead. Both fructified nature by a liquid of life. And the passion of both was celebrated in drama.

In Greece Dionysus' fertility-cult is much more noticeable than his death-cult. This is, however, there. He was the god in whose honour Athenian drama was performed. Comedy emphasises fertility. Tragedy, though this is much disputed, belongs, in part, to a death-cult.[7] The characters are normally the illustrious dead. They wear masks, which elsewhere denote a man representing a spirit; this being the origin of our white-faced clowns. There was in front of the Greek stage, in the middle of the orchestra or dancing-floor, a small altar called by a special name, a *thymele*, which has been supposed suitable for offerings to the dead. Many tragedies included as an incident the appearance of a great character's spirit. Parallels point the same way. Chinese and Japanese plays are clearly based on the dead: in China actors come on by a door called 'the door of the spirits'. An apparently remote parallel is nevertheless very persuasive. All over Africa Africans practise a kind of spiritualism. It is normal for African mediums to dress in imitation of some respected former chief, and to let what purports to be his spirit speak through them. Obviously this practice approximates to a drama in which the actors deliver wisdom from the past, and from the other world.

Dionysiac religion in Greece asserted the strength of life, here and hereafter, for Dionysus always rose again. But, like most of the other early evidence which exists, it does not communicate information concerning the life expected by the Greeks after death. We have various reports (pp. 63, 73 above) of astral travel, or projection, and it would seem that some of those who experienced it must have brought back information about the exact nature of the planes which they had visited; but we are not told what the information was.

These four movements or mystery religions amounted to secret societies concerned with a life after death. They have been investigated separately. But they do not merely touch one another here and there by chance. It is now realised that they all grow out of a similar layer of belief and practice. They are all variations of fertility-cult and death-cult occurring as usual, or as always, together. They were started by people to whom the other world was known and was important. It has been said that all religions begin with an in-break of the world of spirit into the world of matter.

It is at least clear that during the sixth century B.C. many Greeks had come to disagree with the simple Homeric theory that the dead all lived, strengthless, in an underworld, to which all went automatically except a few whose divine connexions earned them happiness in an earthly heaven, and to believe instead that they could all earn for themselves an airy life of happiness after due reincarnations.

The Dionysiac religion was based on direct experience and at least in the beginning some of it was psychic experience. Whether Orphic doctrines came directly is more uncertain. They may have been excogitated on a basis of imported opinions. But a number of Greeks were at least conscious, or said that they were conscious, of former existences on earth. Pythagoras was, or did. There are also plenty of examples elsewhere. In fact, it has been said that reincarnation is the universal belief of the human race except for a few centuries in Western Europe, and even here the poets have generally believed in it. The belief, then, among the Greeks may have originated, as it originated among many or most other peoples, by direct experience. To credit diffusion from some single source with the widespread occurrence of this notion would be placing a heavy load on diffusion.

8   *Early Philosophers*

Soon after the emergence of Orphism came the emergence
of Greek philosophic thought and speculation. That the earlier
Pre-Socratics on the whole harmonise more with Orphism
than with any other kind of religious belief is obvious enough,
but has not been emphasised as it should be. Many of course
were chiefly interested in physics. But several took it for granted
that the nature and fate, here and hereafter, of individual souls
was a necessary subject for inquiry. The contrast with the early
poets, Archilochus (eighth to seventh century B.C.), Alcaeus
b. *c.* 620 B.C.), Solon (*c.* 640—soon after 561 B.C.), and Sappho
(b. *c.* 612 B.C.), is impressive. They belong to a different world
from these poets; but they share their world with Pindar (518–
438 B.C.). And he, and they, are in turn to be contrasted with the
great tragic poets and orators of the great Attic Age. Their
true successor was Plato (*c.* 429–347 B.C.).

According to Choerilus of Iasus (third to second century
B.C.), Thales, active early in the sixth century B.C., believed in
the immortality of the soul.[1] F. W. H. Myers refers to him as
one 'who defines demons as spiritual existences, heroes, as the
souls of men separated from the body'.[2] He was known to
maintain that there was no difference between life and death,
and when asked why he did not therefore die, he replied 'Because there is no difference' (Diogenes Laertius, I, 35). Heraclitus
(*fl. c.* 500 B.C.) is too obscure for certainty, and for him it is
rather the elements than the individual things which they con-
stitute which are indestructible. But even Heraclitus sometimes

seems to contemplate a long destiny for human lives. Like Thales, he was ready to regard 'life' and 'death' as interchangeable terms. 'The immortals are mortal, mortals are immortal, living the death of the one, dying the life of the other' (Fragment 62, Diels-Kranz).

Of Xenophanes (*c.* 570–*c.* 478 B.C.), Parmenides (born *c.* 515 B.C.), and Epimenides (sixth century B.C.) there is more to say, and it is positive. Their systems might be said to pre-suppose psychic doctrines in harmony, though sometimes a loose harmony, with the Orphic doctrines. Pythagoras is more obscure; but if anything is true of him it is true that he held psychic doctrines, including the doctrine of reincarnation.

These thinkers and visionaries believed in morality, or even asceticism, as the price of progress for individuals. Epimenides in particular proclaimed that an individual soul, after due incarnations, might achieve perfect purity and live with God. He claimed to have lived many lives (Diogenes Laertius, I, 114) and to have been instructed in sleep by gods, or spirits.[3] He is also said by Cicero (*De Divinatione* I, 34) to have pro-phesied like a sibyl, in a frenzy.

Empedocles (*c.* 493–*c.* 433 B.C.) was not a teacher only. He had other remarkable powers. He was a political leader trusted to the point of reverence. He was good at solving practical problems. He was a healer of great personal power. He was, if the word is appropriate in his period, a scientist. He was also a poet. He was religious, and believed in ritual obser-vances, and asceticism. At the end of his life he disappeared. There was a legend that he jumped into Etna (Diogenes Laertius, VIII, 69). It has, however, been seriously supposed that, like Enoch (p. 43 above), he was miraculously translated (Diogenes Laertius, VIII, 67–9). That this can happen and could have hap-pened may be argued, but that is not to say that it did.

It is probable that Empedocles had some of the peculiar sensitivity not infrequent at his time. He may well have been directly aware of former incarnations,[4] and seems to have thought that he was living in his last (Fragment 146–7, Diels-Kranz). He

F

may certainly have received communications from spirits concerning the nature of the universe and the destiny of man: at one point he definitely thinks of himself as a *daimon* (Fragment 115, Diels-Kranz). This is not to disparage his own constructive thinking in cosmology, physics and psychology. His two principles of Love and Strife, Attraction and Repulsion, are perhaps obvious, or suggested by Heraclitus. But his emphasis on Love—for as Aristotle noted, his preference for the positive principle is clear[5]—though it did not come from observation, seems to be more than a hopeful guess.

Of Pythagoras (born *c.* 570 B.C.) more is sometimes said; but less is known. Aristotle and Plato knew much about the Pythagoreans but it happens that there is little good and early evidence for the beliefs and discoveries of Pythagoras himself. However, to doubt that he firmly believed in reincarnation, transmigration of human souls into and out of animal bodies, and also asceticism is scarcely reasonable even on the evidence which exists. He was immensely progressive, especially in his theories of mathematics and music, and a very great thinker. He was a humanist in a good sense, with a respect for all life, in which however he retained some old-fashioned taboos, such as we meet in Buddhists and Dr. Albert Schweitzer. His school was as much a monastery as a school. His belief in the spiritual world was characteristic of his age, in which very many men with the ablest minds, which is saying much since they were all Greeks, scarcely thought of confining their acts to the common concerns of earthly life, and confidently proclaimed the future life of human souls after death (Diogenes Laertius, VIII, 36; Porphyrius, *Vita Pythagorae*, 19). The contrast with the belief in a restrictive Hades, a belief never in any sense confined to Homer or even the Greeks in general, and which still, of course, continued, is very great.

There was, therefore, in early as in later Greece, a conviction shared by many that the soul has a future, and that it depends on the life lived on earth. Such a belief is characteristic of the Orphics and many distinguished people who would not have called themselves Orphics. It may have owed something to foreign influence. It certainly owed something to direct contacts across the line between life and death.

Herodotus (v, 92) has a story about Periander, despot of Corinth, who about 600 B.C. lost his wife Melissa. She appeared to him, very angry because he had allowed her to be buried without sufficiently splendid clothes. Periander paraded all the women of Corinth ostensibly for a special religious celebration. They wore their best dresses. He took them and burned them as an offering to Melissa. This satisfied her.

Such a story was characteristic. There was, however, a sharp distinction, as now, between those who accepted the reality and relevance of the other world and those who not only did not, but were scarcely even aware of the alternative outlook.

9 Pindar
Greek dramatists

Central in this whole question is the great poet Pindar (518–438 B.C.), who comes second only to Plato among Greek classical writers in descriptions of the world beyond.

Pindar's Victory Odes include a wealth of mythology belonging rather to the Dorian and even the pre-Homeric than to the Homeric tradition. Pindar celebrates victories in the games, and he recounts suitable myths, suggested by the occasion. Often enough the suggestion is obscured, half-lost in the mythological wealth which it introduces. However, he sometimes draws a moral, or drops a hint, personal to the victor whom he celebrates. And in a handful of passages he reveals his own belief in an effective after-life of rewards and punishments, combined with a doctrine of reincarnation. In so far as such a theology can be called Orphic, and it is roughly covered by what was loosely meant by Orphism, Pindar can count as a convinced Orphic himself. He was most aristocratic; clearly Orphism was not only for the less important people needing consolation. Pindar's other world is poetic. He gives thoughtful pictures of it. He steps into the now familiar tradition of word-pictures representing Heaven and Hell which begin for us in Homer and Hesiod and had been followed and much enriched by several 'Orphic' poems, perhaps many, which are obscure and hard to reconstruct but certainly existed and included such material. Pindar found words in what he heard and read to express his own beliefs. He was clearly convinced, and wanted others to be convinced.

Pindar has several allusions to the after-life. His beliefs agree, apparently, with doctrines in mystery religions. But his eschatology is not narrowly sectarian. It rather represents a more general system of doctrines from which the specialised doctrines of the sects grew. Pindar varies. He tells the story of Castor and Polydeuces, known in Latin as Pollux, the two brothers or half-brothers of whom one had only a mortal nature but the other was a son of Zeus. He, therefore, would be allowed to live on Mount Olympus with the Gods after dying. But he wanted to save his brother from a mortal's death; and it was agreed that both should spend their time in both places, Olympus and Hades, changing over every half-year (Pindar, *Pythian Odes* XI, 60–4; *Nemean Odes* X, 49–91). Now Castor and Polydeuces may be honestly Greek. They have Greek names. Their odd destiny is no doubt a reflection from two Asiatic deities, who lived alternately on and below the earth, no doubt representing the alternation of summer and winter. But for this, it would have seemed very strange that a Greek hero, not of divine descent, should be allowed on any terms to live with Gods on Mount Olympus. The Greek form of the myth has a noble motivation. The divine half-brother sacrifices half his own Olympian life to rescue his human half-brother. Zeus, affected, granted his wish.

This admission to the Heaven on Olympus is unique for a mortal of purely mortal descent, except for the comparable favour accorded Homer's Menelaus (p. 48 above) who was of divine connexion by marriage to Helen.

Pindar has his own Heaven, or Elysion, for those who have lived righteously, while the wicked endure fearful sufferings. His belief is set out in the second Olympian Ode, addressed to Theron of Acragas:

Wealth, bearing an embroidery of virtues, affords opportunities for doing both good and ill. Wealth inspires the urgent zest for adventure; it is a bright, conspicuous star, a true and glowing light for any man. But this is so only so long as he who is rich is aware of what will be; how, when we die in this world, immediately our helpless souls pay their due penalty, for there is one who, below the earth, judges the sins committed in this kingdom of Zeus, pronouncing sentence according to awful and inflexible law; but the good enjoy a life which is without suffering, having sunshine equally in their days and in their nights, and troubling neither the earth nor the sea with hard labour of their hands in a life of penury.

All who have loved to keep their word are happy in days unspoilt by tears, dwelling with the honoured Gods, while those others endure an anguish on which none could bear to look. And there are some who, during three lives in that world and three other lives here, have been strong to keep their souls spotless from unrighteous deeds; these have made the Way of Zeus to the Tower of Cronos. The ocean-breezes blow where the Isles of the Blessed are. There is a blaze of golden flowers, some on dry land borne by bright, lovely trees, and others nurtured by the sea. Chains and chaplets of these flowers they entwine in their hands, and they live by the upright counsels of Rhadamanthus, whom Father Cronos, husband of Rhea enthroned above all others, keeps by him in readiness, seated at his side. Among these, the Blessed Ones, are numbered Peleus and Cadmus. Thetis, the mother of Achilles, brought him also there, after winning the heart of Zeus by her prayers: that Achilles who brought low Hector, Troy's impregnable pillar, whom no other could overthrow, and sent to their deaths Cycnus and the Aethiopian, Son of the Dawn.

In my quiver, under my arm at my side, are many swift arrows, and they have voice for those who can understand, but for those who do not they need one to interpret them. He who has much knowledge as a gift from nature is a poet; you others, who know only what you have learnt, may chatter in endless garrulity, like crows compared with the divine eagle of Zeus, but all to no effect. Come, Spirit in me, hold your bow aimed at the mark. Whom mean we to strike this time, as we let fly from the mind's sensitive part the arrows of our praise? At you, Acragas, shall I stretch the bow. My thoughts are truthful, and I shall speak as I have sworn to speak. I say that not within one hundred years has any city borne a man with heart more intent to do good to his friends, of more lavish hand, than Theron. But envy overtook his praises, in opposition most unfair, for it arose from wanton men, inclined to loud talk, and seeking to suppress Theron's share in the fine acts of good men. The grains of sand are beyond the reach of any counting; and no one can ever say how many joys Theron has given to others.

(For the translation, see p. 20 above)

Though he lays this stress on virtue, Pindar also seems to think that those who win through to his Elysion should be important people, kings or other leaders. Plato thought that rulers were the people with the best chance of going to Hell. Probably most Greeks, if asked who would go to the human Heaven of Pindar, would have said that they were those who had been initiated into the Mysteries.

Pindar is among the rather few great and famous poets who state something like a systematic spiritual or even spiritualistic belief, instead of only allowing such possibilities to emerge as possibilities suggested, but not asserted, by their incidents and imagery. When we remember that a great deal of occult experience and paranormal powers and occurrences was characteristic of the period into which Pindar was born, it is hard to doubt that much of his knowledge came to him, or to someone near him, directly. Of all poets he is most explicit in his trust of inner voices.

The fifth century was the age of the great Athenian tragic poets, and the fourth the age of the great Athenian orators. It is strange but true that among these two mighty groups of exalted writers the signs of a confident belief in an after-life, and the kind of knowledge of it which so many other Greeks of this, and of an earlier, time possessed, are of the scantiest.

On the whole Pindar's great contemporary, Aeschylus (525–456 B.C.), and the other Attic stage-poets leave the other world poetically obscure, concentrating on this one. Divine control, prophecy, evil and sometimes good ghosts and spirits occur. In the *Choephori* (22 ff.), Clytemnestra sends Electra with offerings to Agamemnon her husband whom she had killed, because there are signs that he is angry—or more angry than usual. In Aeschylus' *Persae* (681 ff.), a ghost is evoked from a tomb. It is the ghost of the last Persian king, Darius, who brings counsel and warning for his son, the reigning king, Xerxes, who is letting himself be defeated by the Greeks. It has been argued that tragedy originated from a death-cult (p. 78 above and note);[1] but the outlook remains Homeric in sharply distinguishing the weakness of shortlived humanity from the eternal strength of the divine. A reader can often think that these poets accept the dreary Homeric Hades as all that can be expected. Yet Aeschylus was initiated at Eleusis, and hinted references to Eleusinian beliefs have even been found in his text.

Sophocles (*c.* 496–406 B.C.), in a choral ode of blinding splendour in the *Antigone* (332–64), perhaps the most famous of all his choral odes, having expressed awe at all the other immense achievements of the human mind, ends by saying that one problem remains unmastered, the problem of death. Yet Oedipus in the *Oedipus Coloneus* himself passes to immortality, to become a hero and helper of mankind. Here Sophocles imagined an active protective life of a hero who through suffering has earned life, with power, beyond death. Oedipus becomes a guardian hero. The creation of a hero may have been a frequent subject of Greek tragedy. Perhaps it was originally a principal ingredient. In extant tragedies it is not often the main interest.

Euripides (*c.* 485–*c.* 406 B.C.) left two dramas relevant to our purpose: the *Alcestis*, wherein Heracles rescues the heroine from Death, and *The Bacchae*, a central document on the worship of Dionysus.[2]

Aristophanes (*c.* 450–*c.* 385 B.C.) in *The Birds* provides a brilliantly funny sketch of Socrates holding a séance and calling up spirits—it would be truer to say, letting spirits come—by the edge of a lake or pond, counting as 'the waters of death' for his purpose:

> Beyond the navigable seas,
> Among the fierce Antipodes,
> There lies a lake, obscure and holy,
> Lazy, deep, melancholy,
> Solitary, secret, hidden,
> Where baths and washing are forbidden.
> Socrates, besides the brink,
> Summons from the murky sink
> Many a disembodied ghost;

And Pisander reached the coast,
To raise the spirit that he lost;
With a victim, strange and new,
A gawky Camel, which he slew
Like Ulysses—Whereupon
The grizzly sprite of Chaerephon
Flitted round him; and appeared
With his eyebrows and his beard,
Like a strange infernal fowl,
Half a Vampire, half an Owl.

(1553–64)

So, according to the most eloquent and resourceful, but very expansive and free, translation of J. H. Frere, sang the Chorus in Aristophanes' *The Birds*. They are saying that Socrates called up spirits, and furnish contemporary evidence for this suggestion about him. The notion of an evocation comes readily to Aristophanes as a basis for delightful jokes. Pisander was a vain, overdressed, and cowardly military commander. His spirit had sunk so low in battle that he wanted to 'raise' it; the double meaning of Frere's translation does in fact fit the Greek.

Aristophanes was at least sufficiently interested in Eleusinian and Orphic beliefs to parody them, and indeed to write serious poetry in which 'mystic' belief is remembered. In *The Frogs*, while making fun of Dionysus himself when he seems to be taking the way of initiates into the world beyond death, he yet writes reverently of the actual Mysteries.[3]

But these poets seem on the whole and most often to think that their task is with this world, and that they should not look far beyond. Even Socrates in Plato's *Apology of Socrates* (29 A–E) is made to give the possibilities of an after-life in a simple choice, guided by common-sense without direct information.

Socrates was considered by some others, but not by himself, as one of the Sophists. They, perhaps remembering the traditions of some Ionian physicists, tended to a critical materialism. The great Attic prose writers of the period, especially the orators, were not materialists, but they seem to be quite sceptical about a future life. To them it was myth and poetry. They, rather strangely, do not seem to consider it as a subject on which many Greeks had thought themselves well informed. There may have been religious or social objections; gods seemed to oppose such impiety, and anyway educated people neglected old wives' tales.

IO *Plato and Aristotle*

There was nevertheless a tendency among the finest minds, all the way down to Socrates (469–399 B.C.) and Plato (*c.* 429–347 B.C.), to believe in an after-life. Even Democritus, in the fifth century (*c.* 460–*c.* 370 B.C.), who was the founder of the atomic theory of matter and a materialist, used to spend the night in a cemetery to see what happened.

In Plato's *Apology* Socrates leaves the question open, arguing that even if death meant annihilation it would still be a good, like a dreamless sleep. But if it be a migration, as some believe, to another existence, the gain will be yet greater. In the *Phaedo* he is, according to Plato, emphatically for survival. The *Phaedo* contains an extended description of the soul's destiny beyond death[1]; and, at the Dialogue's close, when himself at the point of dying, Socrates, asked how he would like to be buried, replies, 'Any way you like—if you can catch me.' At the heart of Plato's philosophic system lies the assumption of eternal life, with many incarnations, for the spirit of each individual, agreeing with Empedocles and Pythagoras, or at least 'the Pythagoreans'.

Socrates was sentenced to death and died in 399 B.C. Plato lived on until 347 B.C.

Plato's myths are almost an encyclopaedia of what had been, and might be, fancied on these matters. For Plato the soul survives death, and immediately goes to a judgement. The survival of the dead, and different classes of the dead, was of great importance in his system. In many of his 'myths' he goes into detail concerning it. He tried all kinds of geography. The out-

lines are Orphic or Pythagorean, with lavish and detailed and
often varied imagery.

Those who had died had to be where they could remain
both unnoticed and also safe from encroachment by some
other class of the dead. He finds places beneath the earth's
surface, and other places deeper down. In another passage he
locates some on the other side of the globe, underneath, in
the Antipodes. There is also the old, traditional, place, far to
the West. And there are also locations in the sky, higher, or
lower.

For Plato, spirits are normally eternal. They live before
and after each reincarnation in some place not visible to human
beings on earth. Their fate depends on their moral life, and also
on their own choice. A spirit may choose to be incarnated as a
despotic ruler or tyrant. If so, his position may lead him into
great sins, hardly to be avoided; in such a position with its
freedoms and its compulsions, 'aitia helomenou', 'the responsibility
is inseparable from the choice' (Plato, *Republic* 617 E).

In the *Republic* Plato finds a good way to introduce his mag-
nificent description of the unseen world, and the divine domina-
tion over human life, the place from which we come and to
which we go, and the powers, and the eternal justice, to which
all that lives is subject. He tells the story of a soldier, Er the
Armenian (x, 614 B–621 D). He fought in a battle, and was
wounded and left for dead. But after several days he revived.
His soul had left his body and gone to the other world. All that
Plato has to say of the other world in this passage is given as the
account which Er gave of his experiences. We cannot really
doubt that this important case belongs together with all the
visits to Hades. Part of its great interest is that it is nearer to
direct experience, and not developed so far into pictorial myth
as the numerous poetic versions.

These Platonic doctrines are mainly a development from
the views of early spiritualistically inclined philosophers. They
are in approximate sympathy with the views of the mystery
religions and their initiates who expected a heavenly after-life,

either because they were initiates, or because they were righteous, or both. Plato (*Republic* 364 B–365 A) derides charlatans, itinerant wizards who may sometimes have claimed connexion with the Mysteries; but he clearly admits the validity of true Mysteries, even if he places all or almost all the weight on moral living in highest purity. But Plato's myths, his pictures or even literal descriptions of the world beyond this, have little in common with the myths of the Mysteries. In general all revered the mystery religions, whether or not they had been initiated. But word-pictures of the other world, and the schemes for its arrangement in space, need not be very like anything known to have been in the Mysteries.

Plato's is a majestic demonstration of what can and will be done by a determined thinker and poet who has not at least some rough physical theory allowing for different modes of existence to occur in the same place at the same time without sensibly colliding. But his fantastic framework allowed him his mighty enunciations, and they convey truth. Souls survive, and are schooled. Repayment is made. Souls are eternal. They may develop and develop and rise high. Plato consolidated and more than consolidated the gains of the Greeks and gave them to Neoplatonists, to early Christians, to others, and to us.

Among the short Dialogues which look like Dialogues of Plato but are not actually by Plato is the *Axiochus*, perhaps written in the first century B.C. The Pseudo-Platonic Dialogues are lively pieces. They are inclined to take some notion of Plato from one of the authentic Dialogues and develop it, perhaps going farther than Plato would have gone.

Axiochus is soon to die, and is greatly distressed. Socrates consoles him, interestingly. There is a straight and simple assertion that the dead wake up to a new and blissful life of enjoyment with no unpleasant ingredient to mar pleasure: all is bright and beautiful and there is no more hard work, but only artistic and philosophical engagement, for interest and enjoyment, not for competition and applause. This is for those who have lived good lives, inspired by 'a good spirit', clearly a 'Guide' or Guardian

Angel. The impression is that this is for nearly everyone. There is no thought of reincarnation, as there is more than once in Plato. In describing his 'Earthly Heaven' or Etheric World—he has already written of the desire of the soul to rise to 'the aether' —the Pseudo-Plato writes of the natural beauties there and the easy life and pleasant conditions in terms not unlike Pindar's in the *Second Olympian*.[2]

Platonism impregnated the ancient world, though many thinkers reacted from it; among these not least Aristotle or 'the two Aristotles, the follower and the critic of Plato' (384– 322 B.C.). Aristotle is said to have been present at a psychic experiment on a boy. A 'soul-extracting wand', *psychoulkos rhabdos*, was used; and we wish we knew how. The boy fell into a trance, his soul went away, and on its return it, or he, 'reported each thing'; and again we are tantalised by the brevity.[3]

Aristotle himself seems to have believed in the survival of the minds of individuals, but hardly of individual minds, and certainly not of individual personalities or spirits. His beliefs about the soul's survival changed, or he held different beliefs together incompatibly: the soul pre-existed and will survive; the soul dies with the body and nothing survives; and the soul and body die, but the mind survives without interests or affections, or any personality; perhaps, as some passages of the *Metaphysics* would suggest, as part of the divine reality. He thought that there was something in the mind's more mysterious recipiences, but also objected, and his objections are amusing. If the gods wanted to send such messages, why do visions come so often at night, and so seldom in daylight? Again, if they really wanted messages to be communicated, surely they would have used men of exceptional intellect as recipients (*De Divinatione per Somnum*, 464[a] 19–22; and for further comment on visions in the darkness see *De Insomniis*, 462[a] 8 f.). Perhaps he might be respectfully criticised for choosing the more impossible of the apparent impossibilities open for his choice. He might have accepted the facts and tried to find out why darkness and simple-minded mediums are best for communication. His objections underline the increase of knowledge or at least the change in belief since Aristotle's time. We are no more surprised if spirit-messages come best in the dark than we are that a dark room is needed for developing photographic films.[4] Nor do we now confuse psychic sensitivity with intellectual development, which may even interfere with it. We also know that women are more 'prophetic' than men. So did Socrates, who trusted Diotima rather than any male informant (Plato, *Symposium* 201 D–212 B). Heraclides Ponticus (*c.* 390–310 B.C.), student of Plato and associate of Aristotle, was no sceptic in these matters.

But this is the question, whether in the ancient state of knowledge, the survival of the dead, their messages, and their visibility were scientifically conceivable. Some admirable theoretical work was attempted, forecasting, indeed, modern physics. There was almost a theory of waves, like disturbances in water or air, to account for supernormal appearances (Aristotle, *De Divinatione per Somnum*, 464^{a}6). Alternatively, a movement of atoms was postulated, by Democritus. Both theories might perhaps render the apprehension of non-material spirits more easily credible.

Plato did not experiment. Democritus (p. 91 above) had already experimented. He, the founder of atomic theories, and, we suppose, a materialist, was deeply interested in reports concerning ghosts. He even made what experiments he could, in particular waiting in cemeteries, in order to test his own sensory impressions (Diogenes Laertius, IX, 38). He tried to find the truth about what may have been astral travelling, which was near to the very puzzle which embarrassed Plato. How far he got is not known. But he made his atomic theory account for apparitions by saying that bodies could throw off films of light atoms which could travel and impinge on the senses of people far away (Plutarch, *Quaestiones Conviviales*, 734 F).

He spoke of an emission of particles; Aristotle of disturbances as of waves in water or air. Aristotle, or whoever first thought of the metaphor from waves, deserves immense credit for it. It is strange that these two competing formulae, forecasting the dilemma of modern physics, which is said to waver between these two ways of describing experimental facts, are first met in an argument about ghosts.

What the Ancients needed was a further step such as the modern theory of atomic quanta. Colonel H. R. Dixon-Smith, in a lecture given in London,[5] explains the coexistence of our material, etheric and astral bodies in terms of atomic quanta. Material atoms are each of Quantum X, etheric of Quantum Y, and astral of Quantum Z. No material atom can have a quantum of any value but X; and so for the others, also. Thus there is no paradox whatever in the interpenetration of bodies existing in different modes. Ghosts and a spirit-world need no longer be considered anomalies in nature. Such explanations can help modern man to accept given facts without inhibitions. We no longer need to be like the little boy who, shewn a giraffe by his father, turned round angrily and said: 'I don't believe it.'

11

Summing up
Mazes
Hellenistic Period

One mythical form persists and is very general. It is the journey to Hades, no doubt of prehistoric origin, for Gilgamesh, perhaps rather unemphatically, performs it, and continuing through Homer, Vergil, Dante and Milton to novels of the twentieth century.[1]

There are various forms. One is the journey to a western land. It is unobtrusive in our record, since it so often appears in realistic and literary shapes that do not actually force an esoteric reading. It is clear and direct in the Egyptian version. The dead have to cross the Nile to the western side. It is actual and literal. Gilgamesh travels over a sea, but the voyage itself may perhaps not be westward, though probably the general direction of his whole journey is. Odysseus and Aeneas certainly go west. Their stories demand this; both are to be at home in a western land. The fact remains that they do travel to the West.[2]

The other main form of the death journey is upwards. The beginning is again early. Siberian shamans seem to go upwards in travel to a world more real, and more—apart from very quaint animal symbolism—divine, than the world of earth. The Babylonians have a story of a certain Etana who was carried up to heaven by an eagle to live with the gods, surely an origin for the Greek Ganymede, who was carried up to Olympus at the orders of Zeus by Zeus' eagle. Early Greek philosophers already think of human spirits soaring to the sky. In the *Iliad* the Heaven of the Gods, though it was not for men, is on Mount

G

Olympus, but already in the *Odyssey*, and perhaps even in some parts of the *Iliad* (e.g. VIII, 18 ff.), it seems to be in the sky.

Of the descents to Hades there is much to say. The notion that life comes from Mother Earth, and returns there, is primeval. It is clear in early-style cultures, such as that of the Australian aborigines. 'From the earth come all good things and to the earth they return' is a Phrygian epitaph, '*ek gēs eis gēn tagatha*'. In Greek mythology Deucalion and Pyrrha had to repopulate the earth after the Flood by throwing over their shoulders 'the bones of their mother'. The bones were stones. They threw stones, and the stones became men. There is a theory that the words are cognate in Greek, *laas* being 'stone' and *laos* being 'a people' (Apollodorus, I, VII, 2; Pindar, *Olympian Odes* IX, 43–6). There is also a theory that the very word 'initiate', clearly meaning something like 'allow to go in', originally connoted 'into the earth'. To be initiated people had to enter the earth ceremoniously.

In any case, the 'Descents' were entries into the earth, and some were composed by exponents of mystery religions. There was at least one 'Orphic Descent', and there were probably more.[3] A passage from one of these may have been taken by Homer to be altered and shaped for part of his Eleventh *Odyssey*, where the first part is a kind of séance but develops into what seems more like a visit to Hades.

There was a strong traditional compulsion to retain the underworld journey, so strong that those, for example the modern Malekulans of the New Hebrides and the ancient Romans, who wished to include a bright sunny, flowery, Heaven in their myth, put it sometimes, puzzlingly, under the earth, with of course its own source of light, since the sun in the sky could not be seen underground. To avoid these paradoxes further progress in physics was wanted, but was not available. The Egyptians found no difficulty in supposing that the sun, in his boat, travelled back to the east each night, going underground, where he could give light to the lower world. The Homeric Greeks both did, and did not, follow this conception. For them, too, the sun had to travel back below ground. He did not give light to

Hades. But once, when annoyed, he threatened to do just that: 'I shall go down to the land of Hades and I shall shine among the dead' (*Odyssey* XII, 382–3)—to the Greeks a monstrous abnormality.

In effect, the fortunate dead pass through a dark place where the less fortunate stay, or through a tunnel-like descent. It is believed by many now among those who accept psychic evidence that the passage from life to death is indeed like a dark tunnel.[4] Beyond, both to these contemporaries of ours and to some of the ancients, there is a bright world of pleasant country scenery, with flowers more beautiful than on earth, and life without working for a living. Such is the picture presented by Pindar (*Olympian Odes* II, 61–77; cf. Fragment 114, ed. Bowra). Presently, in the fourth century B.C., the mystic Heaven, following a general trend, seems to be in the sky. The initiated human spirit, after death, has to say, according to an inscription on gold plates found in graves in south Italy and Crete, that his race is 'of the starry sky' even though he has been a man on earth.[5] After all, already in the *Odyssey* the Gods live in the sky rather than on Mount Olympus as, with a few exceptions, in the *Iliad*. Meanwhile, there is Hesiod's lovely account of the good spirits, who have finished the earth-life and travel about the world, noting good and evil deeds, and helping those who deserve help. They have become, says Hesiod, good *daimones* (pp. 53–6 above).

This is a word of very great interest. It seems to be derived from *daio*, 'I divide'. A *daimon* is 'he who apportions'. Presumably at first it was a spirit who allots experiences to men, and controls their prosperity and adversity, not some dim, remote power, but just such a spirit as Hesiod conceived, not far off from a guardian angel. The meaning soon expands and comes to vary. It is often just 'luck'. In the *Alcestis* (499–500) of Euripides, Heracles says, 'This is typical of my *daimon*, my luck. It always goes uphill and is a rough road'. A spirit or guardian angel is hardly a rough road always going uphill, but luck may be. So too the Roman *genius* which each man had was a kind of destiny controlling his luck (e.g. Horace, *Epistles* II, ii, 187 ff.). It was far less personal than the Greek *daimon*, and had complications. It was born with its owner, but it was also a kind of continuity, transmitted in each family. If things go well without accidents, the *genius* is helping. If a man keeps missing easy shots, or falls down in the road, or fails in any purpose, his *genius* is *not* helping. A man would actually sacrifice to his *genius*. There are many parallels to these guardian angels in control of luck: the Egyptian *Ka*, the ancient Persian *Fravashi*, and the modern East African *Mulungu*[6]— they say 'This is just my *Mulungu*', as Heracles said 'This is my *daimon*'—meaning 'my usual luck'.

There seems to be a development or devolution. People begin with spirits, and then, perhaps because they become less sensitive to them or come to mistrust them, try to transform them into some vaguer force such as luck. It is a variation of this process when Homer regularly attributes incidents and accidents and unplanned occurrences to the intervention of a full-scale God. Homer has gods and mortals. Though he sometimes calls his gods '*daimones*' (e.g. *Iliad* I, 222), he in effect almost ignores all the orders of beings in between which have so greatly affected most of the human race (but see also pp. 55–6 above).

Such is one of the sidelights on what the ancients, among others, thought about the interaction between the dead and the living, and an example, too, of how the simple, primeval, acceptance of ghosts and spirits regularly becomes enfeebled, and the facts obscured. Meanwhile the old embarrassment appears. The dead go to a dark place under the earth. Some of them go on to a bright heaven under the earth. But they cross a bourne from which supposedly no traveller returned. However, returning spirits did intervene in the lives of people still on earth, though Pindar thought that they no longer had to work for a living. There was a famous picture of the world beyond by Polygnotus(*fl. c.* 475–447 B.C.), in the Lesche at Delphi (described by Pausanias, X, 28–31). It shewed rewards and punishments.

Most Greeks thought it safest to bury the dead with full ritual, to render them simple but reverent food and drink offerings, and to entertain them to a feast on an annual All Souls' Day, as in the Athenian Anthesteria (the Chinese have a soul-feast where special spoons are provided for those ancestors who have unfortunately been decapitated[7]). At the end of the Greek Anthesteria they said, 'Go out, spirits of our fathers'. The Roman word for spirits is '*manes*', 'the good people', and the Greek '*kēres*', who are pictured as little flying, insect-like creatures, perhaps akin to the butterflies thought to represent the spirits of the dead on the Mycenaean 'Ring of Nestor' (p. 43 above), and elsewhere in the world. Now Homer has *kēres*, but they are not spirits of the dead. They are forces, perhaps little devils: there are *kēres* of death hovering over Sarpedon and Glaucus (*Iliad* XII, 326–7), so that, life being so uncertain, their only choice was to fight bravely. Elsewhere (*Iliad* XVIII, 535–7) men are threatened by a deadly *Kēr*, in the singular. No doubt like other words such as '*daimon*' the word '*kēres*' had at first meant 'spirits of the dead', but the meaning was later obscured, though it survived unquestioned at Athens.

The spirits had to go back to their place. They were wanted to stay there, except on special conditions at special times, a quaint and familiar ambivalence. There is reason to think that the well-known pattern of the maze,[8] offering a path from outside to inside and from inside to outside to those who know the way through, belonged especially to the relegation of the dead in their proper place. The pattern, and this application, are well spread about the world. They occur in Egyptian tombs. The same principle is active in the Chinese 'spirit-walls', a sequence of barriers at the entrance to a Chinese city like the baffle-plates of a petrol motor's silencer. The megalithic Male-kulans of the New Hebrides in the Pacific, who have very interesting death-myths, place emphasis on mazes, of which they have a rich variety in their dances and plastic designs besides their myths. In one myth especially the spirit of a dead man walks along a sea-shore till he comes to a cave. There there is awaiting him a 'guardian ghost' called Temes Savsap who has with her half a drawn maze-pattern. The spirit has to complete the pattern by drawing the other half. If he does, he is admitted to the land of the dead inside the cave. If he fails, Temes Savsap eats him. This myth comprises, all in their proper places, the elements of a widespread old-time belief. There is a sign of it in a megalithic chambered cairn at Bryn Celli Ddu in Anglesey, where the entry is a spiral path recalling the delaying effect of a maze. Maze-like patterns were till lately drawn on doorsteps in Lancashire, no doubt to entangle unwanted spirits. There is much more to say. But for the present it is enough to mention an astonishing parallel to the Malekulan myth in classical Italy, divided from it by thirteen thousand miles and two thousand years. Here, in the Sixth Book of Vergil's *Aeneid*, the hero Aeneas, like Homer's Odysseus, goes down to Hades while still alive to meet his deceased father Anchises. The entrance is at Cumae near Naples. He lands on the coast near by, visits the temple of Apollo, and sees on its gate, and is delayed by, the picture of a maze in the form of the Cretan Labyrinth represented with all its story, engraved by Daedalus himself. He next enters the Sibyl's cave and receives her prophetic directions. After that he passes through a cave to the lower world.[9] In Vergil's 'Descent' there is again a dark tunnel, with varied occupants there and in adjacent places. There are certain kinds of Purgatory and Hell. And there is a bright Elysion beyond for the elect, reached, as among the Malekulans, by passing down into the earth.

All this is implicit rather than explicit in the records of classical antiquity. The history of the maze-motive, beginning in spirals of the full neolithic period in Asia and some of it spreading to the Mediterranean area from secondary centres of diffusion in north Europe, possibly joining with a stream of influence from Egypt, is a tale of a primary importance, and shews its rich results in mythic imagery. The relation between life and death coloured thought. The clearest example is the legend of the Labyrinth in Crete. 'Labyrinth' seems to mean 'the place of stone'. A labyrinth was at first a stony cave, the entrance to the body of Mother Earth, where the dead might go to their home in the mother from whom they came. Such is the thought which led to the practice of burying the dead crouched in a pre-natal posture, as if ready for rebirth, a practice well known and lately reported from the newly discovered neolithic remains of the once-fertile Sahara, while in South America hut temples are actually formed, as are some stone European graves, in the shape of a womb.

It might not be obvious why a cave should be connected with a maze-pattern. There is however sufficient proof. A labyrinth is called, for example, spiral, 'snail-like', and there are other ancient descriptions which are explicit enough. Indeed, 'labyrinth' is the ancient word for 'maze' and there is no other, except —very strangely indeed—'Troy'. The great principle is the severance, but not the total severance, of the worlds of living and dead. The severance must be both an obstacle and a path, exclusion and also conditional penetration. The pre-eminent effective symbol of this is a spiraliform maze. At a ritually important cave-mouth the pattern could be formed by a maze-dance, and indeed traces of such a dance have actually been found associated with palaeolithic cave settlements in France. The principle could be applied in architecture. Egyptian tombs are built to enforce a path of many turnings. The Egyptians, and the Chinese who constructed 'spirit walls', may well have thought that spirits could only fly straight; and anyway earthly enemies, including tomb robbers, might be hindered by confusing turns.

The name 'labyrinth' could be applied to any mortuary building, as if signifying the whole. Pliny mentions two such 'labyrinths', the famous Egyptian example at Hawara which, as Pliny notes, was said by a certain Lyceas to have been a mortuary building, and which had a large complex of many underground rooms; and the much more obscure 'Tomb of Lars Porsena' in Etruria (Pliny, *Naturalis Historia* XXXVI, 84; 91 f.). No doubt both were somehow well arranged to keep out the unwanted. Almost equally obscure is the Cretan Labyrinth

at Cnossos. Here the great palace can easily be supposed to have
been the labyrinth, perhaps called so because later Greeks,
knowing only the ruins, thought their confusing complications a
sufficient reason.[10] But there is plenty of evidence that the palace,
before its destruction, was labyrinthine. It was contrived to
have obstructive twists and turns, so that according to Vergil
(*Aeneid* VI, 18–30), Daedalus, the builder of it, taking pity on the
captive Theseus and the princess Ariadne, gave Theseus a
thread to unwind as he went in and to follow as he came out.
It is firmly recorded that the Cretan Labyrinth worked like a
maze, and it is probable that some part of it was built like a
maze. There was probably a magic ritual in which performers
actually went in and out, expressing perhaps many things, but
including the continuity of life.

The name 'Troy' or 'Troy Town' belongs to mazes in many
places, especially in northern Europe including Britain. Such
mazes were ritually 'trodden', in what Shakespeare calls a
'Nine Men's Morris':

> The nine men's morris is fill'd up with mud,
> And the quaint mazes in the wanton green
> For lack of tread are undistinguishable.
> (*A Midsummer Night's Dream*, II.i.98)

Nine, by the way, is a symbolic number for death in ancient
Persia, Italy, Ireland, and no doubt many other countries. It
was a case of who should go in and how anyone could come
out. So it was in the great fortress of Homer's Troy, with its
powerful walls and well-designed gates. It, too, presented a kind
of maze-problem. Indeed there are hints that a magical maze-
dance may have been performed at the gates. Vergil says that when
Ascanius or Iulus, the son of Aeneas, was founding the city of
Alba Longa, he performed round it 'the Trojan Ride' (*Aeneid*
V, 596 ff.), that is, evolutions on horseback certainly following
the lines of a maze-dance, for Vergil explicitly compares them
to the Cretan Labyrinth.[11]

There is one more link. A maze goes round and round like

the spring of a clock or the entrails of a human or animal body. The inner parts of Mother Earth were so imagined, and so were, actually, the bodily parts of Hades himself, this time meaning not the place but the king of the dead, '*en enkasin Hadou*', 'in the entrails of Hades' (*Anthologia Palatina* xv, 40, 42). There is a strange clay object, made in Asia Minor about 1000 B.C., on which is the maze-form apparently constituting an architectural edifice, with the legible words in cuneiform, 'the Palace of the Entrails'.

There are two comparisons. At Epidaurus, the great Greek centre of healing, possibly including spiritual healing or even faith healing, there was a round temple, and in the centre of its foundations, a circular maze of masonry, allowing a passage to the centre. There is a maze, also architectural, newly discovered at the site of the Oracle of the Dead in Epirus. This maze is actually in a part of the precinct which has been supposed to be used for spiritualist operations, perhaps séances.[12] The separation between the spheres of existence would, if so, have been neatly signalised. Part of the meaning may be the wandering of a soul on the way to peace. We are told (Lucian, *Cataplus* XXII, 644) that there was a blind march of those to be initiated on the way to the vision at Eleusis, and that it was a wandering way. So, on the way out of the Cretan Labyrinth, Daedalus guided the 'blind footsteps' (Vergil, *Aeneid* VI, 30) of Theseus with his thread.

Grave-inscriptions should be useful evidence for beliefs concerning death and the life beyond. They are disappointing. Earlier examples are austere, giving little but names. Later, feeling and sentiment appear, but little assurance of anything but the brevity of life and the pathos of death. There is also cynicism as in the famous and frequent use, both in Greek and in Latin, of the words: 'I was not. Then came to be. I am not. No effect on *me*.'

More and more the form taken is an appeal to passers-by —graves were placed beside roads—asking their interest or pity or even some favour.

As time went on the learned and the unlearned views on the after-life separated out, at least for a time. Many people tacitly assumed what has been regarded as humanity's universal non-Christian belief, the belief in an underground Hades, with souls only half alive. There is not much to shew from the Hellenistic Age—roughly, the second and third centuries B.C.—nor indeed from the half-century before it; the whole period between Plato and Cicero has little that is arresting. There are few if any reports of inbreaks from a psychic world, as in the generations from about 600 B.C. The influence of Plato himself, and therefore of Pythagoras and perhaps others, rose and fell but never entirely ceased. There continued to be speculation, especially among Stoic and Epicurean philosophers, concerning the place of the spiritual in creation, and there was also a continuation of mystery religion, Orphic perhaps, but possibly a little generalised. The inscribed gold plates found in graves in southern Italy and Crete prove that many individuals were assured of a bright survival, perhaps in a starry heaven (p. 99 above, and note 5), a striking development to which Eastern speculation had contributed. Posidonius (c. 135—c. 51/50 B.C.), a Stoic thinker and writer of a productivity near to genius, certainly left the door open to a sane acceptance of survival and indeed an active spirit-world. Meanwhile Pythagoreanism and Platonism formed a new and most important current, the current of Neopythagoreanism, lively in, or behind, the works of Cicero, and leading on to Neoplatonism and a large part of Christian doctrine.

The long stream of Greek debate, some of it shadow boxing, went on for centuries. The period of scepticism did not last. There was a steady, or an impulsive, flow of Eastern influence, conveying sometimes suggestions, sometimes experience, and sometimes superstition. Fantastic magic came, much astrology, and much attention to the air and the sky as a location for an after-life. The name 'Gnosticism' covered a great volume of this thinking. Gnosticism is little respected. The bad extremes were certainly bad. But the good side, whether called Gnostic or not, contained high and pure and true religious knowledge. Later the paranormal was sometimes accepted by the Churches, especially the Eastern Orthodox Church in which many saints and clerics displayed a special knowledge and special powers.

12 Romans: General Introduction

These were the centuries of Roman emergence. Rome, battered by every impact from outside, stubbornly developed, as one among many Italian agricultural communities. True Italians, the Italici from the north among whom the Romans are to be counted, had a simple, primitive-looking, belief. It is the belief, fundamentally, of farming people, appropriate to the village rather than the city; it may be derived from some common system generated by tribes of Indo-European speech whose descendants included Celts and Teutons. In Roman belief the dead survived, but of their new life scarcely anything was known. They were called the '*manes*', 'the good people', a word always found in the plural; they seem to be an undifferentiated multitude, a normal early supposition perhaps characteristic of humanity in general.

The early Italian view of the dead belongs to a very early cultural phase indeed. The name 'the good people' itself appears to be treating the dead with respectful fear. This is an earlier stage than anything in historic Egypt or Sumer. But it is known elsewhere. It is the stage at which individual dead are not distinguished. In pre-Roman times bodies were sometimes cremated, and then the remains were placed in urns and the urns in urn-fields. The urn-fields seem to have been located in front of settlements where the power of the dead could repel attackers. It is only after this stage is passed that individual dead men can be remembered, and possibly promoted to be heroes or a kind of saints or even gods. However, by about 1000 B.C. the graves in the Roman Forum shew that both cremation and inhumation were already practised, indicating two layers of population, and some individuality begins to appear in the siting. Complete cremation has never preponderated anywhere for long. In Greece it is the Homeric method, but as a regular custom it is only proved archaeologically for an early and limited period.

Etruscans appear to have come from Asia Minor to Italy during the thirteenth century B.C., and another wave in the eighth or seventh centuries. There were plenty of impacts from outside; Greek gods reached Rome before about 500 B.C. Italy had many streams at different stages of development attempting to coalesce. A fully 'deistic' culture more than once broke into 'manistic' conditions, or conditions not far beyond the 'manistic'. These conditions by themselves tend to develop into a religion of ancestor-worship (p. 60 above). In Africa something like this change has been seen developing. For centuries no one was remembered. Then some great chief attained the privilege of being remembered and respected, for many generations. But as the generations passed memories of different chiefs coalesced. The originally remembered chieftain collects attributes belonging to his successors. He begins by lasting as himself only for four or five generations. More generations pass, and he collects attributes from successors. They are forgotten. He continues to be remembered, but does not slip farther back into the past. He is always thought to have lived three or four generations ago. He might become an important element in the growth of a God.

Thoroughly characteristic of the Romans was their rigid state control of religion, which must have started well before history became reliable. The Roman Senate and priesthood wanted all things prescribed and unalterable. They wanted the dead to be respected and celebrated in cults and festivals, and the great dead to be revered and remembered. They did not want an easy daily intercourse with the dead as among ancient Egyptians and Getae, and modern Bornese and, generally, Africans. It is perhaps partly through the fear of such intercourse that the Senate fiercely opposed the religion of Dionysus, and even the doctrines of Pythagoras, when books by him were said to have been dug up, and were ordered to be burnt (Livy, XL, 29; Pliny, *Naturalis Historia* XIII, 84 ff.).

Almost equally characteristic of the Romans was a long, indeed almost an infinite, list of 'functional deities', tenuous existences, whether spirit, force, or dim neutral conception, supposed to exist each for one single operation. Levana, for example, was the 'goddess' of the father's act when he ceremonially lifted up his new-born baby and so acknowledged it to be his own. The act was done. Such deities existed, satisfied the act, and ceased to exist, all in a few minutes. Whether in any sense they existed or were thought to exist when not on duty is obscure. In rather the same way the *manes* themselves could be forgotten for most of the time.

The *manes* were at first not in any sense individuals. They were the dead in general, who lived in tombs, and who guarded each tomb. Their cult was a soul-cult. Then they were probably considered as particular, but not individual, dead people, belonging to the tomb which they guarded. If so, a cult of ancestors became possible. The term *di parentes* and the festivals of the *Parentalia* and *Rosalia* have been thought developments which began after the conception of ancestral *di manes* was reached. Presently there are actually *manes* of individuals. So it is in literature. The *manes* are first ghosts of the dead, then ghosts of ancestors, and then, still in the plural, a single ghost of a single dead individual. Cicero (*In Pisonem*, 16) says *coniuratorum manes mortuorum expiare*, 'appease the ghosts of the dead conspirators'. That is still not one individual. But when Propertius (III, i, 1) addresses *Callimachi manes*, he must mean the single ghost of the individual Callimachus, and when Livy (III, 58, 11) talks of *Verginiae manes*, he must mean Verginia's ghost.

The *manes* are an obvious start for exploring Roman ideas about death, because the notices about the *manes* prove that the Romans in general believed in a life within or beyond the grave. The belief was not detailed or precise. There was room for speculation, but there was not much tendency to speculate. The

Romans were busy with the duties of this life, which was usually hard for them. Their epitaphs, however, shew that they regarded death with strong feeling. Two kinds of feeling are emphatic: one is pride, and the other is affectionate pathos. The epitaphs of Scipio Hispanus and his great predecessor shew a strong interest in family honour and achievement. Those who sustained the Republic, and their own name, gloriously, seem to have felt safe in the care of their ancestors.[1]

Left to themselves, the Romans, and other Italians, might have done very badly indeed in contributing suggestions concerning an after-life. Unlike Homer, they thought that the dead required to be remembered, at least collectively, in festivals. Like Socrates' accusers they did not want to hear about them, or get in touch with them. They did not, like Wang Ch'ung in China in the first century A.D., say that ghosts and spirits are mere fancies due to human folly: they had words for ghosts and spirits, and anxiously kept out of their way.

But the Romans were not left to themselves. From about the earliest suggested date for the foundation of Rome, 800 B.C., onwards, Greeks began to form settlements in Italy and Sicily, and the Etruscans, if not all round and indeed inside Rome, were just across the way. The Greeks had plenty to offer, experience and speculation. They spread Orphism, or a faith like Orphism, up Italy, a version of Orphism perhaps affected by Pythagoreanism which appears in Greek Campania, in southern Italy, in the fourth century B.C., as is proved mainly by the inscribed gold plates found in graves (p. 99 above, note 5).

The history of Italy and her invaders provides room for many different outlooks. The Etruscans belonged to some old Asiatic tradition. They, like the Egyptians, firmly believed in a future life, and rewards and punishments in it. At first, as their pictures shew, they took a balanced view, and thought about a happy land below the earth where a new arrival, travelling sedately in his carriage, is welcomed and feasted by his waiting relatives. But they became rather morbid in emphasising a hell to which bad men were to go, and the controlling demons, especially

Charun, a development of the Greek ferryman of the dead, Charon. In late Etruscan paintings the emphasis is rather on hell than heaven. They were forecasting, or supplying with material, the Middle Ages and Dante. On the whole, the Romans ignored this, except for a passage in Plautus (*c.* 254–184 B.C.) where painted scenes of Hell or Purgatory, no doubt Etruscan, are mentioned (*Captivi* 998 ff.). Of course, they took much else from their neighbours, especially Etruscan augury, of Babylonian type, and gladiatorial games.

Etruscan belief spread far, from the Po valley to Rome, Latium, and Campania. It is a permanent background to much of Italy, and is a more than usually explicit recognition that life continues on the other side not very different from life here, and may be very full and enjoyable. The belief belongs to religious tradition and may be a long way from any folklore origins which it may have had somewhere in Asia.

There was, however, a notable cluster of meanings, some spiritual and perhaps psychic, round one traditional nodality among the Romans. They provided themselves with a king, following Romulus, called Numa Pompilius and said to be a Sabine from the small town Cures. His date ought to be from the end of the eighth century onwards. But the Romans said that he had been taught by Pythagoras. In saying so they were about a century out. Numa, if he existed, was far earlier, as Cicero and Livy protested.

But Numa may indicate a reversion to what might be called a personal religion. One of the legends makes out that he used regularly to visit a nymph called Egeria, and she instructed him (Livy, I, 19). Her name might mean 'She who extracts', and it has been easy to suggest that she 'extracted' secret knowledge, possibly by a medium's faculty. The Romans were very ready to trace their religious system to Numa. It has been said that all religions have been started by personal psychic experience, such as clairvoyance, and the rest. The experience may seem to come in dreams, which have regularly been granted high authority.

In the Hellenistic period, the great State Cults of Olympian deities weakened. Individuals relied on the mystery religions, of which some existed in Asia beyond the Greco-Roman world, or worshipped human individuals such as Ptolemy in Egypt or Demetrius Poliorcetes in Athens. It is hard to say what new inbreaks, if any, there were from another, psychic, world: Numa and Pythagoras belong to the earlier period, when many such inbreaks are reported. The Romans may have been extreme, but need not have been abnormal, if they accepted a kind of personal revelation as the basis of their religion, and from then on sought rigorously to oppose any more revelation. This might have come, of course, from the Cumaean Sibyl, the famous prophetess at Cumae near Naples. She is described as very much like a medium, as many other sibyls were, as described by the great philosopher Heraclitus himself, who noted violent signs, no doubt of possession and control, in a sibyl of whom he knew (Plutarch, *De Pythiae Oraculis* 6, 397 A). The Romans said that an early occupant of the sibylline cave came to their king Tarquinius Priscus, offering him nine prophetic books. He refused. She returned saying that she had burnt three but he could have the remaining six at the same price. He refused again. She came back again, having burnt three more. This time he did buy, at the original price, the three remaining (Dionysius of Halicarnassus, IV, 62). The story may be absurd, but it does indicate, not without humour, the very restricted and cautious Roman approach to any mystery, especially any psychic mystery. They kept the books carefully. They appointed special officials, at first two and later more, to guard them, called 'The Committee of fifteen officials in charge of the sacred rites', *quindecimviri sacris faciundis*. These officials consulted the books, and reported what they found there, when, and only when, instructed by the Senate to do so, always in some crisis.

All this may not seem relevant to beliefs concerning an afterlife. But it is at least marginal to them. If such prophetic people as sibyls prophesied, they could, according to those who are intimate with such matters, have done it in different ways.

H

They could have been directly aware of the future in some such manner as that explored by J. W. Dunne, the writer of the famous book on dreams, *An Experiment with Time*. Or they could have seen clairvoyantly and heard clairaudiently spirits of the dead who, 'seeing a little further along the road than those still in the earth-life' as the formula is, could tell them the future. Or they could have gone into trance, and accepted possession, or rather 'control', by the spirit of a dead man. If this is impossible, it has at least seemed possible to many thousands, or indeed millions, of people, ancient and modern.

Plautus (*c.* 254–184 B.C.) wrote a play, the *Mostellaria*, which is supposed to mean, near enough, 'The Haunted House'. The usual young man of comedy, left in charge of the house during his father's absence, turns it into a gay, perpetual nightclub, all drink, love and merriment. On his father's return, he kept him out of the way by pretending that it was haunted, and for a while succeeded. But the ruse was discovered by the father. There was a row, but eventually they became reconciled. This is a Greek story, told in, and probably before, the third century B.C. Haunting certainly was known, and there are a handful of stories about it, not very many, but some, and one or two in several different versions. The most famous, in at least three versions,[1] is about two travellers who arrived at Megara. One, A, stayed with a friend and the other, B, at an inn. In the night A dreamt that B appeared to him and said that the innkeeper meant to murder him. A nearly went to his rescue, but decided it was all nonsense, and went back to sleep. Then B appeared again, and said, 'As you failed to rescue me, please give me a proper burial. If you will be at the city gate at dawn, you will find me covered up in a wagon and being smuggled out.' A, this time, obeyed. He intercepted the wagon, found the corpse, and arranged for the burial of the friend and the punishment of the killer.

An intriguing story is related by the younger Pliny (*Epistulae* VII, 27). There was a haunted house at Athens. The haunt brought the price down. A philosopher, Athenodorus, bought it, moved in and started writing. Night came on, and so did the ghost, an old man with fetters on arms and legs. It beckoned and moved away, followed by the philosopher, finally disappearing in the courtyard. The philosopher marked the spot, and next day reported the occurrence. Digging at the marked place unearthed a fettered skeleton. It was properly buried, and the haunting ceased.

It is hard to know how old these stories are. They may have been copied and re-copied often before they appear in the text from which we elicit them. They belong, however, to well-known types. The stories are told at many different times because the experiences in them took place at many different times. It is quite certain that all such reported occurrences in medieval and modern times cannot all be merely repetitions from an ancient tradition. Some allusions, however, which seem to date them, need not necessarily do so. The fetters might seem to prove at least a metal-age date. However, a stone-age ghost-story might have survived into a metal age and then acquired, in the telling, these metal-age appurtenances. The strong argument is, that the ghost-appearances have been so well attested by precise and trustworthy witnesses at so many different times and places that, firstly, at least some must be genuine, and, secondly, many, even some which are not so certain, simply because they are so like the others, may be assumed with strong probability to represent real experiences. There exist several classes of appearance: they are genuine and real classes, and at least many of the examples which they contain are genuine and real also.

Phlegon of Tralles (*c.* A.D. 150) tells this story, as based on his own experience (*Mirabilia*, Ch. 1). A young man, Machates, when lodging in a guest-chamber, was visited by a daughter of the house, Philinnion, who had recently died, though he did not know this, and they slept together for a number of nights. They exchanged presents. He next learned from her parents that she had been dead for some time. The parents surprised her during her next visit, and she fell down dead. On exploring her tomb they found it empty except for the presents which Machates had given her. Meanwhile her body had remained in the guest-chamber. It was then reburied with care.

The events in this story need careful consideration. It has been suggested that Machates was a very powerful materialisation-medium, providing psychic strength for Philinnion to use. But as the story goes there is more than that. During this materialisation, on the apparition's visits, or if not then at least afterwards, the bodily remains of Philinnion were absent from her grave. They were found later in the guest-chamber. Only Machates' presents were found in the grave. If these are all true facts, it is hard to see what was done to the body, and why, since there could have been a direct, that is a new, materialisation, the body remaining where it was. Instead we appear to have a revivified corpse, indeed a resurrection of the body, to be classified, even, with the Resurrection of the Body in the New Testament (p. 153 below).

Werewolf phenomena are very strange.[2] Perhaps they should be taken together and not compared with other kinds of occurrence. But the ancient story of the Man and the Soldier, this one retailed by Petronius (died A.D. 65; *Satyricon* LXI–LXII), had better be mentioned here because of the manipulation of a body.

One night a man walked out, to visit a woman, Melissa, whom he loved, accompanied by a soldier. The moon was shining brightly. They reached a cemetery. There, at the side of the road, the soldier took off all his clothes, laid them there, and then they turned to stone. He turned into a wolf, and ran off. The man hurried on in panic to his destination. Melissa said she wished he had come a little sooner, for a wolf had been worrying their sheep. It had escaped, but with a gash in its neck inflicted by one of the slaves. The visitor now set off for home, and on his way back he noticed that at the place where the clothes had been changed to stone there was only a pool of blood. On his return home he found the soldier there, wounded in the neck and attended by a doctor.

There is a widespread type of story to which this one belongs, a type in which a wound inflicted on the animal-form is found reproduced on the human-form. In later versions sometimes a silver bullet is needed to kill the werewolf, or were-hare, or whatever the creature is: I have lately heard of were-jackals in east central Africa. Now though this class of tale is numerous and widespread and some examples are fairly well attested, they are yet too obscure for use in explanation of other recorded phenomena. The body of the werewolf may be dematerialised, and rematerialised as a wolf. Or possibly a different process may occur. The spirits of the dead may be involved, but there is little if any indication that they are. There may be nothing but fancy in the tales. That is unlikely. But whatever the truth may be, there is little chance as yet to make use of it.

14

Cicero
Lucretius and
other poets
Livy

The Roman outlook on an after-life is, however, not wholly simple. The strong religion of the family involved at least some interest in the survival of the dead. At funerals portraits of ancestors were proudly carried: at the funeral of Marcellus there were six hundred litters (Servius, on *Aeneid* VI, 861). The epitaphs shew great pride and much simple pathos. This, combined with the limited belief concerning the *manes*, amounts to some sort of mental picture. Meanwhile there are strange things in poetry, hard to interpret. Ennius (239–169 B.C.) apparently managed to be both a Pythagorean and an Epicurean at the same time, and, at least according to what he wrote, not only believed in reincarnation, but actually claimed to remember some of his own past lives.

Greek influence, classical and post-classical, was already strong at the beginning of Roman literature, which it detonated. Epicurus (342–271 B.C.) died not very long before Ennius was born. Stoicism and Epicureanism were in sharp competition. Neither altogether neglected the problem of the soul and its survival. Epicurus, the materialist, gave a materialistic account of the soul, and was said to have been the first to teach that the soul dies with the body. His statement that 'when we are there, death isn't; when death is there, we aren't' (Diogenes Laertius, x, 125) is however far from pessimistic, and might even be called happily ambiguous. Despite his beliefs, he left instructions for offerings to be made at the tombs of his relatives (Diogenes Laertius, x, 18).

The Stoics were in some difficulty over the question. Some believed in determinism and predictions, and some in free will; or they tried to reconcile these two positions. They thought that the soul survived for a time in a restricted sense,[1] but on the whole had not much to say about the conditions of the other life. But one of them, the distinguished Posidonius (*c.* 135–*c.* 51 B.C.), included in his Stoicism the old Eastern doctrine of reincarnation based on moral achievement; assuming, that is, that he was the source of Cicero's remarkable pages, at the end of his now fragmentary *De Republica*, which give us 'The Dream of Scipio'.[2] Here, Cicero (106–43 B.C.), in a kind of Platonic myth, goes a long way towards a firm belief in a spiritual background for actions and events. Human lives are for testing and for growth. A good life here leads to a happy life hereafter. But we must not hurry to our bliss. Suicide is very wrong, and we must follow our path to the rightful end, obedient to the gods, or rather, as the ancients tended to say in such grave and illuminated moments, God. The great men of Rome are seen in a sky-heaven, caring for their descendants, and happy in what their own will and achievements have won for them. Cicero writes out the tenor of majestic commands from beyond.

Elsewhere in his great volume of writing Cicero quite often shews sympathy with the more positive views. He is remarkable for this, and the first Roman to give us anything explicit. No doubt Plato, who greatly impressed him, was for him a permanent possession and element in his thinking. But clearly he added to the literary texts the direct experience of people known to him.

Cicero, like others in antiquity, used the general conception of prophecy or divination to cover the paranormal. There was a tendency to regard anything strange as a sign from the gods and mainly interesting for that reason. Cicero therefore gives space in his *De Divinatione* to the psychic. The work is a dialogue. In it his brother Quintus Cicero argues that psychic phenomena really occur and he himself, Marcus Cicero, argues that the events

in question have been wrongly reported or misunderstood. It
is all very modern and very much the kind of argument which
takes place now. It is well done too, the honest and broad-minded
application of reason to difficult problems. Cicero's dialogue
rehandles Aristotle's old arguments regarding the dependence
of supernormal perception on an abrogation of daylight
reason and reliance on people of weak intelligence (II, 126; 129;
for Aristotle, p. 94 above). For once we today can claim progress. We use darkness and a red light for photography, and can
use them with equanimity for other spiritualistic purposes
(p. 95 above, and note 3). We have also learnt that recognition
of truth may come 'out of the mouth of babes and sucklings'
(Matthew XXI, 16) and that to man's wisdom the things of God
may appear as foolishness (I Corinthians II, 14). The beliefs of
Quintus Cicero within the dialogue are not affected by such
weak arguments as those of Aristotle.

In another dialogue, *De Legibus* (II, 22), Cicero, in drafting
the laws of his ideal Republic, includes the command: 'Let
men hold the rights of the *di manes* as sacred; let them regard
as gods their kinsfolk who have died.'

He is sometimes very sympathetic. In his *Tusculan Disputations*
(I, 27–29) he said that the pontifical laws and the rites of burial
would not have been so scrupulously defined and respected
without a fixed conviction of the soul's survival. This belief is
likely to have grown from the appearances of spirits in early
times:

The fact is that men, as they had not yet become acquainted with
natural philosophy which first began to be studied many years later, had
only such convictions as they had gained from the suggestions of
nature: they had no grasp of a reasoned system of causation and were
influenced by the frequent sight of apparitions, mostly seen in the hours
of night, to think that those who had departed from life still lived.

(Trans. J. E. King, Loeb Classical Library)

More, he proceeds (30) to suggest that this was the basis for
the belief in the existence of gods. He can conceive of the soul as

existent in independence of the body, in terms of 'air' or 'fire'
(40–1). But he does not believe all the myths. Like the sceptic in
Plautus' *Captivi* (p. 112 above) he regarded the horrors depicted
in Etruscan myths of hell as silly superstition. At times he even
doubts whether you could find a crack-brained old woman so
daft as to believe them (*De Natura Deorum* II, 5; *Tusculanae
Disputationes* I, 48).

In some, if not all, moods Cicero thought augury, prophecy
according to strict rules and rigorously controlled by priests,
had helped Rome. It could be manipulated, to obstruct party
legislation—useful though unscrupulous. But Cicero sometimes
thought that this prophecy really did furnish truth from some
higher source; though he also, as had Cato (234–149 B.C.)
before him, expresses a certain wonder, how two soothsayers
could pass each other in the street without laughing (*De Divinatione* II, 51–2). This prophecy, he says, is 'art', *ars*, that is, a
science, based on knowledge and training. He allows the other
kind too, the kind which is 'madness', *furor*, that is, 'inspiration'
(*De Divinatione* I, 12; 34), obviously the kind practised by sibyls
and some Delphic prophetesses, the kind covered by the Greek
terms such as '*entheos*' which carried with it the lengthened
form '*enthousiasticos*', our word 'enthusiastic'. But he does not
interpret this prophecy as due to a spirit, probably the spirit of a
dead man, controlling a medium. This many now would think
the obvious truth.

Meanwhile Lucretius (*c.* 94–55 B.C.), the great Roman poet
of materialism, whose poem *De Rerum Natura*, almost 'How
the world works', Cicero read and indeed, perhaps, edited,
passionately protested, as a follower of Epicurus,[3] against all
belief in the soul's survival and especially belief in Hell. It has
been argued that there was some official attempt at suppressing
Lucretius and other heretics, if the word is tolerable: certainly
Lucretius was little mentioned in some periods of antiquity.
It is, of course, debated whether Lucretius' contemporaries,
who were Cicero's contemporaries too, really needed such a
violent deprecation as that made by Lucretius, or whether

Lucretius reproduces a situation actual for his Greek sources, but not for him. Plato, and other Greeks, especially Greeks before him, had apparently believed in Hell, but not many educated Romans of the first century B.C. believed in it. Like Cicero, they were inclined to believe in paranormal phenomena, but not in Hell. But the evidence for these occurrences at this time is sparse: whether it was officially suppressed or not is an interesting question. We know that Bacchic religion was suppressed, or at least repressed, and it would seem that, in general, Roman governments believed that the *manes* should be left to the priests. What are so often, in such circumstances, called 'dabblers in spiritualism' may well have been regarded with suspicion.

Yet at the same time other traditions were respected, including the Pythagorean. Neopythagoreanism was alive and healthy. Its exponent among Cicero's friends was Nigidius Figulus, a very learned man to whom four hundred books were attributed. He was fascinated by the occult, engaged in psychic research, and may well be designated a theosophist or spiritualist.[4] It was said that he once used boys in a state of extrasensory perception induced by incantations to describe what had happened to some missing coins (Apuleius, *Apologia* 42).[5]

This period, the first century B.C., includes puzzlingly variant opinions, some held by the poets. Lucretius, passionately materialistic, takes the fear of death and something after death to be an obsession among normal human beings. But though Epicureanism was very fashionable at the end of the Roman Republic, Lucretius' insistent denial of an after-life scarcely had much effect, for he does not seem to have been very much read at any time, and anyway the Epicurean arguments were well known apart from Lucretius' version. The contrary belief may also have been argued persuasively in a poem now lost, the *Empedoclea* of Sallust (probably not the famous historian). It must have reminded some Romans of much interesting material from Empedocles concerning the soul which is not available to us. The Pre-Socratics were not forgotten. Numa Pompilius was believed to have been a Pythagorean.[6] His association with the nymph Egeria has been thought to mean that he regularly received advice from a spirit whom he heard through clairaudience.

Catullus (*c.* 84–*c.* 54 B.C.) evinces little or no hope of a future state:

> *Soles occidere et redire possunt:*
> *nobis cum semel occidit brevis lux*
> *nox est perpetua una dormienda.*
>   (V, 4–6)

'Suns can fall and rise again; but we, when once our brief light falls, must sleep one everlasting night'. Elsewhere (CI) he is frantic before death's stark wall of finality.

Horace (65–8 B.C.) is not frantic, but quietly sad to think that all of us, even the greatest, will one day be only dust and a shade (*Odes* IV, vii, 13–16). He was not otherworldly: he shews us Augustus, in the future, sipping nectar with gods on high after his earthly life, but this is current myth, not close to a basis in experience (*Odes* III, iii, 11–12). The rest, like Aeneas, Tullus Hostilius, and Ancus Marcius, are to be dust and shade. Certainly he leaves out Romulus, supposed to have been translated, and at least allows us to become a shade as well as dust. But he fails to allow even Aeneas his official status as an Italian god. We, he says, following Catullus, are not like the moon, which revives always to live again, here agreeing exactly with a tribal poet of Africa, a rather rare example of such materialism from a less civilised community.

Tibullus (*c.* 48–19 B.C.) is sad, graceful, and without any constructive suggestion. Propertius (*c.* 50—after 15 B.C.), however, is at least a little constructive, and of great interest. He begins with his dynamic love-poetry. Then, disappointed in love, he becomes interested in the majesty of the Roman past, and the Roman present and future. His poetic sense grasps the quality of the Roman character and achievement. From this apprehension he takes another step, not obviously necessary, but seeming to be somehow consequential. He comes to deny that the dead are nothing: *sunt aliquid manes* (IV, vii, 1). He attained a hopeful belief in an after-life to be welcomed rather than feared. His passionate sufferings awakened in him a certain deeper or even spiritual vision.

Ovid (43 B.C.–*c.* A.D. 17) is traditional. His Hades is normal. Death is sad, tragic, a final disappointment. But he is to be thanked for one important passage in which, talking about King Numa in the Fifteenth Book of his *Metamorphoses*, he gives (75 ff.) a short but most effective and beautifully rounded account of Pythagorean doctrine: there is no death, but souls move about from one body to another, human or animal: the rule of purity is absolute; sheep do quite enough for us in providing us with clothing without also providing us with food; life is eternal; some, including Pythagoras himself, can remember their former incarnations, as Ennius claimed to remember his. Ovid's passage, characteristically, looks as if it was included as an amusing curiosity. It is naturally hard to say how authentic it is, but it may not be far from accuracy. Lucian (*c.* A.D. 120—after 180) includes a number of Pythagoreans in his parade of all known philosophers; that is, to him, cranks. These doctrines were firmly held and practised.

Livy (59 B.C.–A.D. 17) allows a certain number of mysterious events to occur in his History. He reports, though without himself subscribing to, Proculus Julius' claim that the spirit of Romulus, who had disappeared in a cloud, had reappeared to him to prophesy the future greatness of Rome (I, 16). Livy seems to believe that the established religion has its own meaning, and is important. But he does not go far beyond it. When his sources give him an interesting occurrence he includes it, as when the consul Publius Decius Mus and his fellow-consul have simultaneous dreams of a majestic figure warning them that victory will depend on a general's self-sacrifice to the *manes*, the shades of the dead. Decius Mus heroically follows this counsel (VIII, 6, 9). The sacrifice has a Greek original concerning Codrus, but the story is fully adapted to Roman belief. Livy himself does not shew much faith in any future state.

15   *Vergil*

Vergil (70–19 B.C.) can truly be said to have believed in an after-life if not for every minute of every day at least most often. As Professor T. J. Haarhoff says, he was a peculiarly universal poet.[1] He was also a poet who fully attended to the world of matter and sense, not a mystic with eyes only for the beyond. He probably had some kind of special sensitivity. Vergil both makes death the traditional sombre mystery of epic and also shines a bright light of revelation on to it. But he wrote his poetry by psychological rather than psychic methods. He read immensely, and allowed his poetry and thought to grow out of innumerable reminiscences, combined together to form new expressions carrying new meanings. The new meanings always or nearly always agreed with his judgement in so far as any judgement could be independent of the poetic statement. Thus, if he says that the good go to Heaven, it is because he chose to use words derived from literary sources, which, as he re-combined them, came to mean this. It is also because he himself really thought so, whether through direct experience or guess-work or some other means.

Already Vergil, and Horace also, accepted a sky-heaven for Augustus when he should be dead and deified. Julius Caesar had been deified, and possibly Vergil's Daphnis in the *Eclogues* represents Julius. In any case Daphnis' elevation to heaven, whoever he may be, is interesting (*Eclogues* v, esp. 56 f.). It is an unusual picture, for the time. The deifications of Julii come unexpectedly, in a Roman context, but not if seen as a continuation of Hellenistic deifications. Vergil soon enough, in the *Georgics*, imagined Augustus as due to be deified. But both the *Eclogues* and the *Georgics* are of this world, and face the hard facts of the reign of Jupiter. At the end of the *Georgics* Eurydice goes back to Hades, and Orpheus, having saved her once, cannot save her again (*Georgics* IV, 502–3). It is the world of tragedy, which has to be careful of letting a future life's consolation dilute the intensity. Yet before this in the Fourth *Eclogue*, combining, characteristically, Etruscan prophetic doctrine with an inversion of Hesiod's Five Ages, Vergil had imagined a golden age, an earthly heaven to come, in which men, heroes and gods mingle together (*Eclogues* IV, 15–16); a free intercourse which, undeniably, may and probably does represent the normal conditions of some tribal societies such as the Bornese and the Masai, who are in normal daily contact with clearly seen spirits of their dead.

Vergil's language has what has been called an 'apocalyptic majesty'. He, if any one, could surely see the tier on tier of the world's spiritual structure. Certainly, he does not leave us uninformed. His whole universe is instinct with the active Divine. It is, as always with Vergil, interesting to note not only what he says, but also what he does not say.

He always appears to follow literary tradition; and, with the stupendous learning proper to his epoch and still more to himself, there was no lack of literary tradition to follow. This might seem not worth saying. But it is. Vergil's obvious use of literary sources is often taken to mean that he has little to say himself, and only provides what is second-hand. This view is quite wrong. Vergil profoundly and intricately makes his sources help him to give his own message and nothing else. Such is the simple truth; the full statement of what he does is very complicated, but not essential here.[2]

There is another consideration. Vergil says what he himself means, but, helped by his sources, fits it into, or on to, the existing tradition. In the eschatological passages of his poetry he all the time indicates that what he is saying is what Homer,

Pythagoras, Pindar, or Plato might have said if they had gone a step forward or had had the opportunity which lapse of time had given to him, Vergil, their inheritor.

In Vergil's Fifth *Eclogue* Daphnis the shepherd becomes a god and lives after death in the sky. In the Sixth *Aeneid* his hero Aeneas, guided by prophetic advice, goes down into the cave at Cumae near Naples, and finds himself in the world beyond death, where, in some degree, Hell, Purgatory, and Heaven—Elysion—are revealed to him, and he meets his dead father Anchises, as Homer's Odysseus had met his dead mother Anticleia. In the Eighth *Aeneid* the picture is supplemented by a further Vision of those who suffer in the Beyond for their sins (*Aeneid* VIII, 666-9). The Sixth *Aeneid* is central, to Vergil's eschatology, to his poem, and perhaps to all non-Christian religious history: it comes near to being central for Catholicism too.[3]

The 'Descent' begins by an approach to Apollo, who is allowed full control, and to the Cumaean Sibyl, who is called priestess of both Apollo and Hecate, the Diana of the world below. Vergil might be said here to be reconciling free prophecy with organised, religious prophecy, the contentious issue already at least suspected to be real even for Homer, and already plain in the prehistory of Delphi. Apollo brings free prophecy, ecstatic, inspired and mad, as Cicero calls it (p. 122 above), 'inside the Church', where it can be watched, and interpreted. Characteristically, Vergil retains the old, and reconciles it with the new.

This is where the labyrinth appears, the maze-like gateway, admissive and exclusive, to the world beyond, reached along a shore, as it still is, among the Malekulans, far away in the New Hebrides. At Cumae, however, it is not a mere maze. It is an elaborate bronze sculptured door, such perhaps as the still existing bronze door to the Baptistry at Florence done by Ghiberti in the fourteenth century, a noble masterpiece. Vergil's door shews the Cretan Labyrinth, and indeed a rich précis of the whole myth of the Cretan Labyrinth. Athens is shewn, and the lot-

drawing to decide who is to be among the seven young men
who must be sent to Crete to meet the Minotaur, and be sacrificed as reparation to King Minos. Opposite is Crete, with its
'laborious building', the place of 'wandering not to be unravelled';
except that Daedalus himself, who built the edifice, guided the
'sightless footsteps' with 'a thread' (*Aeneid* VI, 20–30).

Aeneas was reading the message of the pictured gates. What
the message of the whole fearful story was, we hardly know.
Perhaps it conveyed some secret of life and death: how to live,
and secure that the transition to the other life will be smooth
and felicitous.[4] However, the Sibyl would not let Aeneas read
on. She peremptorily told him that he should not waste time,
but sacrifice bulls and sheep. This he did. It is as if the Sibyl
had told him not to rely on his own personal explorations and
conjectures, but to continue with customary religious observan-
ces—'not to neglect his church-going' would be a modern
equivalent. She tells him to pray. He prays to Apollo. Only
then can the great doors open; and they do, of their own accord.
Aeneas remembers the warning of Helenus (*Aeneid* III, 441–57)
and asks the Sibyl not to write her prophecy on leaves, as
she often did, for they would blow about, and their message
would be lost (*Aeneid* VI, 74–6). It is as if he wanted to retain the
full content of free, and not institutional, prophecy. And there
is moral cogency also. Aeneas has to find and take as passport a
'golden bough'. This is many things, but it is certainly 'The
Golden Bough of the Divine Plato, sparkling all round with
every virtue', a conception which Vergil derived from the nearly
contemporary Greek poet Meleager (*c.* 140–*c.* 70 B.C.; *Garland*
47–8).

When the Sibyl does prophesy, she goes into a trance after
signs of great disturbance, and clearly Apollo himself controls
her. She is, and behaves as, a medium. She seems larger than
normal, and her voice 'has not the tone of mortality' (*Aeneid* VI,
48–51); all this in sublime Latin, the only language for 'apocalyptic majesty', and in that language at its best. She is in the tradi-
ition of Heraclitus, who centuries before had mentioned a

I

sibyl 'of raving lips' (see Plutarch, *De Pythiae Oraculis* 6, 397A).
Ancient mediums, Greek, Roman and Chinese, and some modern
oriental mediums, apparently made and make very heavy
weather of going into a trance: modern, western, mediums go
off into a trance quite quietly, apart from a little heavy breathing,
except when certain less desirable spirits control them.

The Sibyl prophesies the future of Aeneas, or some of it. They
then go into Hades, a dark, shadowy world, half real. They
pass the spirits of babies who had died too soon, on the threshold
of life, and now surviving on the threshold of death, pathetically.
Those, now, who claim experience in these things would say
that this is wrong. The babies, even those who were still-born,
would have been growing up happily in their world, much as
they would, if they had lived, in ours.

So, too, do others suffer, as we might say, unjustly. Among
them are suicides, those who died for love, and those not
properly buried. They wait, retaining their earth-life's sorrow,
debarred from crossing the waters of death, and from reaching
rest (*Aeneid* VI, 431–44). All this would be called common, or
even normal, pagan belief. In Vergil the unburied have to wait
a hundred years (*Aeneid* VI, 329); he does not here specify how
others are released, but he does not lay it down that they never
are, and later in the book he gives a more thorough scheme, of
regeneration and reincarnation. Dido is more emphatic here
than most of the other spirits. She has not forgiven Aeneas, but
she is happy now with Sychaeus, her former love.

On the way are many symbolic figures and monsters, not solid,
and not fully real, such as Centaurs and Scyllas, and there is a
great elm tree with dreams clustering under the leaves. Elsewhere,
souls cluster, not dreams: there may be here one of Vergil's
characteristic light changes. Aeneas and the Sibyl go on in the
half-light. The watch dog of Hades, Cerberus, is neutralised;
they drug him. A kind of comedy is allowed. There is surely
some when they come to the waters of death, a lake or river
across which the grotesque ferryman Charon ferries the newly
come souls in his wretched, leaky boat, which sinks lower

under the weight of the fully solid Aeneas, who is certainly no light ghost. Charon will only accept the qualified, who do not include the living. But the Sibyl shews him the Golden Bough. He had seen it before (*Aeneid* VI, 409)—we have no idea when, certainly not for a long time—and he accepted it as a passport. They crossed; and eventually dedicated the bough, hanging it up in a kind of archway or door or false door, where Proserpine, the Goddess of Hades, could receive it (*Aeneid* VI, 630-6).

To the left a path leads to Hell, and the Sibyl tells Aeneas a little about Hell, through which, at her installation, Hecate had conducted her—as today it is thought that a medium can sometimes come in contact with 'lower spheres'. Vergil believed in eternal punishment for some great mythical sinners, such as Ixion who tried to violate Juno. Many others were punished, and there is a list of sins which earned punishment. It may well be more probable that there is hope for all souls, unless perhaps for some few who are irreclaimable, and are not punished for ever, but simply dissolved, as in Ibsen's *Peer Gynt* (v, vii). The dissolution seems to be a Chinese thought. Instead of taking an oath, a Chinaman will break a plate and say 'If it is not as I say, may my soul be broken up as this plate is broken up'. That one soul may simply not survive, though other souls survive, is a different conception. The Egyptians thought that the life was in the stomach, and if that was not carefully embalmed the soul would not achieve survival.

Ahead, Aeneas and the Sibyl now saw great ramparts of steel, built by the Cyclopes (*Aeneid* VI, 630-1). They may be part of a very old mythical pattern. The Malekulans believe in a tall fence in the lower world, beyond which is a kind of Elysion.

For Vergil, it is to Elysion (in Latin, 'Elysium') that the road to the right leads; and the travellers walk there. They climb up a slope, and see below them a glittering land. The air is bright and fresh, and Elysion has a sun of its own (*Aeneid* VI, 640-1)—with a memory of Homer's when he imagined the sun, in a huff, going down to shine among the dead (*Odyssey* XII, 382-3), as

of course the Egyptian sun was supposed to do every night.
Pindar (Fragment 114, ed. Bowra) was trying to say the same as
Vergil. It is a problem. The dead live in a different dimension.
That is, they should not normally be in a dimension dependent
for light on the sun, which, like the rest of our world, is in our
dimension, not theirs. They must therefore, and all the more
if they are imagined below the earth, have their own sun,
or some other source of light.

Here, at last, Aeneas meets his father Anchises, as is appropriate
and indeed inevitable. But it is worth noticing that a father who
is to be met fits neatly into the tradition. Gilgamesh meets his
grandfather; Homer's Odysseus meets his mother; Aeneas
meets his father. This is how great poetry works, by the 'chance
which is the friend of art'.

Anchises shews Aeneas souls not yet born but due to be born
in their time and to be descendants of Aeneas. The earlier and
later parts of Homer's book, the Eleventh *Odyssey*, are different
from each other. So they are, but differently different, in the
Sixth *Aeneid*. Here the first part is largely elicited from existing
myth with mysterious elements of history and anthropology.
The later part is based on esoteric material, partly on Pythagorean
and Platonic knowledge, the emphasis being on reincarnation,
not on the old static Hades and Tartarus. Perhaps Aeneas
comes through the delusions of myth to a philosophic and indeed psychic truth.

Aeneas questions Anchises and Anchises answers with a
statement of the universal scheme, the rule of spirit throughout,
and the purification of each individual soul in the spirit-world
by fire, by water, or by the winds (*Aeneid* VI, 724–51). Meanwhile the souls of Romans, while on earth, are to build Rome
and the Roman Empire. They can be seen, looking as they will
look when on earth (e.g. *Aeneid* VI, 760, 771, 779, 788, etc.;
especially the vision of Marcellus, 860 ff.). This is unusual, to say
the least. Prophecy does not often look ahead many centuries
and include detail. Perhaps only Nostradamus went so far. The
Roman souls are as they might well be as affected by their lives

on earth. Those claiming second-sight often claim also to see very recognisable individuals who have lived on the earth lately or long ago. It is not unlikely that Vergil began with a knowledge of this kind of vision, and simply practised one of his inversions, picturing the souls as they might have appeared to a contemporary of his own who was clairvoyant, but casting the picture dramatically back to the days before Rome was.

Anchises' descriptive prophecy of many individual Romans, in the future to him but of course to Vergil himself in the past, is full of heroic universal values, but it is addressed to Romans. His account of the whole scheme of the universe, his cosmology, is addressed to all.

Anchises presents the universe as matter instinct with spirit in every part of it, mind, *mens*, activating the whole of it. There are also individual living organisms, including humans. They have minds and bodies. Their minds are obstructed by their material bodies, these bodies being the source of feelings and emotions, such as fear, joy, and desire. Therefore the minds or true selves, being imprisoned in windowless matter, cannot 'look with wide eyes at free air'. They acquire stains of guilt as they live their lives on earth. They die, and undergo a cleansing process, by fire, water, or windy air. Then they conceive a desire to live again—strictly, being without bodies now, they should be incapable of desire—and are reborn for a further span. After this has happened several times, each soul is left with a purified consciousness: it is 'a spark of elemental fire', and lives, apparently, in bliss for ever. Some attain bliss at once: Anchises says 'we few are admitted to Elysium, and have our home in the meadows of delight'[5] (*Aeneid* VI, 743–4).

The general doctrine is apparently Indian, and Pre-Socratic. It gives a descent of spirit into matter, and an ascent again, after experience, purification and enrichment. Heaven is not a place where, says Studdert Kennedy, 'the sheep-faced angels bleat', but rather for those who, as Pindar said, 'have three times dared' (*Olympian Odes* II, 68), or much more than that, according to Empedocles (Fragment 115, Diels-Kranz): great heroes and leaders who have done and suffered, for whom the trumpets might well sound on the other side. Plato's scheme is immensely elaborated, but the core is the same. Cicero's 'Dream of Scipio' (*De Republica* VI) fits. It was left for the Romans to write freely and at length about conditions in their Paradise.

To judge from letters of the rather later Apollonius of Tyana, or of some other author confused with him in the tradition, the Neopythagoreans already had an extremely coherent and progressive doctrine of life and death, in line with Thales and Heraclitus, who said that there was no difference between them (p. 81 above). But we shall come to this. Romans of Vergil's time were certainly interested. Probably they believed little in the terrors of Hell. If so, they perhaps regarded the terrors in Vergil as poetry not theology. Vergil adheres to epic tradition, however much more he may provide than just that. He accepted, and indeed required for his poem, the tragic side of the heroic. He could not lament a young, beautiful, warrior, cut off in his prime, if he had just been quoting Heraclitus and saying that death did not matter. Meanwhile the sombre part is only a part. Unlike Homer, Vergil looks forward, to a glorious Roman future, making at least much of the suffering worth while. Many things happen in the rest of the poem. But the Sixth Book, in the middle, shews the truth behind the phenomena, the activity of a divine mechanism concealed beneath the material world. The adventure of Aeneas can be regarded as a mystical vision, as astral projection, or even as a psycho-analysis, as if, going into the cave, Aeneas went down into his own unconscious mind to become aware of its contents, perhaps 'the Archetypes', as Jung would say.

However, at the end of the 'Descent' and the visions comes the mysterious, equivocal, conclusion. 'There are two Gates of Sleep', one of horn, and one of ivory. The horn gate offers easy exit for 'true shades'. The ivory gate is shining-white: but the spirits of the dead, the *manes*, 'the good people', 'send false, wakeful, dreams to the sky' (*Aeneid* VI, 893–8). First, Vergil does not say that anything comes through the ivory gate: he says that the spirits send something, itself obscure enough, but he does not say by which way they send it. What they send looks superficially like dreams, *insomnia*. This is a mixed and artificial word, coined by Vergil. He used it in the Fourth *Aeneid* for Dido's fitful, nightmare-ridden, sleep and wakefulness (*Aeneid* IV, 9)—a superb demonstration of sheer poetic might. In the Sixth this same word is used, and nowhere else, till others copied it from Vergil. There is the word *somnium*, 'dream', and a singular word, *insomnia*, sleeplessness, both coming from *somnus*, sleep. But *insomnia* is plural, a mixture between 'dream' and 'sleeplessness'. And this is, or these are, what the spirits send up 'to the sky' either through, or not through, the Ivory Gate of Sleep; and Vergil calls this, or these, false. Finally Anchises sees Aeneas, and the Sibyl, out through this Gate, and not through the Horn Gate of 'true shadows'.

It is tempting to say that here is the subtlest mind in literary history at its most subtle. Vergil is propounding an eschatological doctrine with reservations. There are many possible suggestions. Perhaps Vergil is saying that Aeneas and the Sibyl, or they and their journey, are just a legend, and not facts, Or perhaps they really made the journey, but what they saw and heard was untrue—hallucinations. Perhaps they and their visions were true, but the spirits also send fitful nightmares besides the true evidence represented by Aeneas and the Sibyl. At least Vergil is not emphatically recommending belief in the system which the Sixth *Aeneid* presents.[6] In the earlier eighteenth century Bishop Warburton published a book, *The Divine Legation of Moses* (London 1738–41), in which he firmly stated that 'the masterpiece of the *Aeneis*, the famous Sixth Book, is nothing else but a description . . . of the Eleusinian Mysteries' (I, 182). There is truth in this, though probably nothing in Vergil can be called 'nothing but' anything: there are always different layers of meaning. But, if there is a strong reference to the Eleusinian Mysteries, which were always kept very secret, in Vergil's Sixth Book, it would not be surprising if Vergil subtly indicated, at the end, that, whatever the secret truth of life and death might be, he himself had not revealed it in any guilty sense, or to any guilty degree. He prefaced his description of the Descent with—for him a rarity—a personal prayer: *sit mihi fas audita loqui*, 'may it be allowed to me to speak what I have heard', 'may I be without sin if I speak what has been told to me' (*Aeneid* VI, 266).

The *Aeneid* is an epic, and epic like tragedy needs intensity unrelaxed by injudiciously admitted consolation. The thought world in it is of Homeric shape under Homeric deities. But the movement is a linear ascent, divinely aided and foreshadowed, towards a Roman future. There is a strong and sure purpose, reaching farther than any purpose in Homer. There is also a transcendent sanction. The *Aeneid* is not only of this world. The Sixth Book, with its visit to Hades superficially like many others, Orphic, Homeric, or Asiatic, is Platonic rather than Homeric. Aeneas, led by the Sibyl of Cumae, goes down through the cave by Lake Avernus and sees the souls. Some await burial. Some are punished. Some live in bliss. Some await rebirth. The doctrine is elaborate, compressed from many sources: Plato, Pindar, Bacchylides (*c.* 505–*c.* 450 B.C.), Cicero in 'The Dream of Scipio', Stoic writers, and no doubt very many more. Aeneas sees the future of Rome, and his own descendants who are to make it. He is strengthened and confirmed by the assurance, and has, on the whole, more confidence after it.

This revelation is important, and meant to indicate truth about the world and its divine government. The best traditions of earlier poetry and thought pointed this way, and Vergil consolidated them with elimination and condensation, and presented a still more profound version. It is not all consistent and the exact experience on which one part or another part may be ultimately based is not explicit. The learning used is, of course, vast. But the result is poetry of incomparable mastery and delicacy, minutely precise in controlling the reader's mood and directing his emotions towards right thinking, a miracle of extreme human attainment. It has not Plato's long elaboration of detail. But it has more than Pindar tells. And it has the feeling of the Roman, deeper as some say and more responsible than the feeling of a Greek. It is at ease with its Elysian fields, where souls free from rebirth stay; it does not go with Eastern sages, and with Empedocles or even Pythagoras to the diviner, inexpressible heights; but it asserts the spiritual government of the universe, and the eternity of souls.

In other parts of the *Aeneid* there is some diversity. Earthly life is always short, and 'irreparable'; it is succeeded by an existence among the shades below, or an everlasting darkness, or an iron sleep. That is all, approximately, Homeric. Intense epic or tragic action is better ringed with a hard, unshining, boundary; it is hardly possible if the characters, like the Getae, are only too glad to be killed and go to the happy land beyond. But Vergil is above all comprehensive. Elsewhere, as always partly depending on sources, this time post-Homeric sources both Greek and Latin, he gives some interesting and carefully-thought glimpses. Latinus, King of Latium, consulted the Oracle of Faunus, where the priest, lying on the skins of sacrificed sheep, sees the spirits of the dead floating in the air, and is able to converse with 'gods', who are of course as much 'spirits' as 'gods' in any modern sense; and Latinus himself hears the voice of his father, Faunus (*Aeneid* VII, 79–101). An old Trojan, Nautes, who advised Aeneas to leave some of his company in Sicily and to proceed to Italy with the others, has psychic powers, given by Athena, by which he can precisely interpret any signs of Heaven's wrath and explain what sequence of events they foreshadow (*Aeneid* V, 704–7). There are in the Sixth Book itself lines about the Sibyl as she goes under control which are detailed and express precisely what sometimes, though not always, happens. There are apparitions. A god or devil suddenly appears. Or a mist is shed to conceal a character. Much of this is Homeric, but not less true to fact. Even Homer, when he lets a god withdraw the veil from a mortal's eyes or clothe a mortal in a mist, is, as Professor T. J. Haarhoff has suggested (p. 55 above), not contradicting psychic experience but using memories of it; and so is Vergil, when he, with characteristic variations, applies such motives (e.g. *Aeneid* I, 411–12, 516; II, 604–6).

Often Vergil makes death tragic, sombre, pathetic. Even
Jupiter's own son, Sarpedon, as Jupiter himself recalls, had to die.
Fate is inexorable—though sometimes it seems to be the instru-
ment of Jupiter. 'Cease expecting that the Fates of Gods can be
deflected by praying', the Sibyl commands Palinurus, the helms-
man of Aeneas who had been drowned (*Aeneid* VI, 376). But
important results come from prayers, or deeds, elsewhere.
Orpheus brings Eurydice back from Hades but loses her again;
Heracles stole Cerberus the watch-dog; and Theseus attempted
to abduct Proserpine (*Georgics* IV, 485–558; *Aeneid* VI, 119–23;
392–6). It is all traditional, and of course always used with
poetic effect. There is some reason for the view that Vergil
has two religions and two systems of belief about life and death,
the Sixth *Aeneid* evincing one sort and the rest of the *Aeneid*
another. The Sixth is Platonic: the rest Homeric. Of course
both parts, Homeric and Platonic, are above all Vergilian. But
in fact through much of history there have been two strains,
the religious and the psychic, the church and the free prophet,
the institutional and the spiritual. Usually an individual is
mainly on one side or on the other. Characteristically, Vergil
includes both sides, respects both, and gives us opportunities to
make comparisons, or even achieve some reconciliation, between
these opposite poles.

Early Empire Writers
Lucian

During the early principate superstition increased. Astrology had come from the East earlier, and, though officially opposed, gathered influence. Other Eastern beliefs notoriously flowed into Rome in great volume. They appealed to individuals, whether educated or not, in search of personal salvation. So did the fashionable Stoicism, but mainly to the educated. Stoicism allowed some chance of imagining a future life, which Epicureanism, now going out of fashion, did not. The evidence now becomes very complex. Literature does not offer much at first. It shews that necromancy was practised. Nero himself tried to consult the spirit of his mother whom he had killed (Suetonius, *Nero* 34).

Traditional beliefs survived, often feebly. But grave-inscriptions from various places in and outside Italy are not confined to them. Some say scarcely anything. Some even express a hope that the departed may be seen in sleep or vision. Some picture him rising to the stars for a divine life, or joining in a feast of the gods. There was, perhaps in Syria especially, a considerable development of these conceptions. Mankind did not give up hope altogether.

There was even a revival of psychic powers. In Egypt they were habitual, and Egyptian influence spread. There were many 'mystery religions', supposed to give a new strength of life, here, or here and hereafter, to their initiates, perhaps especially the Mysteries of Isis, trusted and admired by Apuleius (born *c.* A.D. 123). The magical papyri contain much nonsense and some evil.

But they shew that many people thought that they could make contact with the dead, and liked to do so.

Spiritualism, as it can frankly be called in this context, became a serious and widespread practice, and a subject of debate. The psychic factors in earliest Christianity have no doubt been exaggerated, but they are certainly extremely important. In Palestine under Tiberius there was a violent outbreak of un-paralleled power. Our Lord was undeniably a very great master of psychic, as of spiritual, power. The miracles are not mere legendary impossibilities, or a defiance of the laws of nature, but an extreme use of those laws, which may be classified by reference to well-attested modern phenomena.

The 'Silver-Latin' age of the first century A.D. includes two poets who are of immediate interest. Statius (*c.* A.D. 45–*c.* 96), in his long epic the *Thebaid*, accepts and elaborates traditional myth concerning the after-life. He has his journey to Hades, and other approaches to the dead. But they seem to have a force and colour beyond mere mythology, and suggest that there is more than mere myth in Statius' mind and experiences (*Thebaid* IV, 406–645). Lucan (A.D. 39–65), in his epic *The Civil War*, usually called the *Pharsalia*, strangely avoids myth al-together. He writes of the war between Caesar and Pompey, and his characters are historical characters. He represents and denounces the horrors of civil war and mass destruction; and he deals with fact rather than fancy. He has two important passages about the after-life. In his First Book (I, 452–62) he finds occasion to mention the Gauls, and proceeds to describe their beliefs rather as Herodotus described the beliefs of their cousins and predecessors the Getae of his time, the fifth century B.C. (p. 77 above). Lucan's Gauls want to die, being confident that there is happiness in death. Of their Druid priests he writes:

To them alone is granted knowledge—or ignorance, it may be—of gods and celestial powers; they dwell in deep forests with sequestered groves; they teach that the soul does not descend to the silent land of Erebus and the sunless realm of Dis below, but that the same breath still governs the limbs in a different scene. If their tale be true, death is but a point in the midst of continuous life.

(Trans. J. D. Duff, Loeb Classical Library)

Lucan's other important passage on death and the after-life is in his Sixth Book and is about necromancy (*Pharsalia* VI, 569–830). Pompey seeks a prophecy about his future. He goes to a witch in north Greece, and she revives a soldier killed a few days before. The soldier, in his earthly body, arises and speaks a prophecy of doom. There is considerable detail. Apparently the soldier has not much time. His revival is only possible before his body decays, not after.

All this, the Gauls who 'go rejoicing to their happy hunting ground in the west', and the necromancy, is rather ancient than modern. But some direct experience may well be indicated. There is, however, no suggestion yet of the grave, scientific, mystical and highly progressive explorations of the Neoplatonists.

The ensuing Latin writers of pagan antiquity have not much of what is here called direct experience to report. However, Seneca's discussion of odd occurrences and their possible explanations, a discussion not unlike Cicero's, certainly indicates that there were ghost stories and other such curiosities.[1] But these writers, relying on their old classical tradition of the relief and repose and restoration to be found in literary art, found no golden key. Even the Christian Boethius (*c*. A.D. 480–524), in terrible stress, wrote his *Consolation of Philosophy* (p. 177 below), in which he profits from his literary and philosophical knowledge and art, and from his moral will and will to worship God, with little or no reassurance that the great consolation is to come after death.

There was however a positive outburst of psychic revelation, both Christian and Pagan, to be found recorded in Greek works, written by Greeks and foreigners. In the middle period, about A.D. 160, Lucian's brilliant mockery alone is overwhelming proof that much was going on which might attract mockery. But even in spite of it Lucian is inclined to let through some hint of a genuine practice or belief. He treated spiritualism as he treated the philosophical schools, as if there were little or nothing in it; he judged beliefs according to his sharp and humorous perception of the human weaknesses, especially small-minded vanity and little dishonesties, of their exponents. He mocks a certain Peregrinus who made a great display of dying on a pyre with an assurance of surviving death, someone who apparently wanted to end as Empedocles had been thought, though probably incorrectly, to have ended (Lucian, *Peregrinus*, *passim*). Peregrinus himself must have believed. Through another contemporary, Alexander of Abonuteichos, perhaps, as Lucian depicts him, the greatest charlatan in literature, even greater than Browning's Mr. Sludge, Lucian seems to be parodying some kind of reality. Alexander carefully contrives a special kind of trumpet for what is today called the 'direct voice' of a spirit (one not coming through a medium's mouth) by using for this the windpipes of dead cranes and an unseen accomplice (Lucian, *Alexander or the False Prophet* xxvi). There is conveyed an impression that 'direct voice', so imitated, might still be a real possibility. The conclusion is that some people honestly believed that they heard the direct voice through trumpet-shaped instruments specially provided, quite honestly. Plenty more might be found. When Lucian writes of a séance, it may be funny but is not necessarily nonsense. When the spirit of Homer 'returns' and says that he was not born at any of his reputed birthplaces but was in fact a Babylonian, it is funny in the context, but it still looks like a parody of some occurrence seriously supposed to have happened.

The great psychic revival of the early centuries A.D. seems to have emerged in many places, and at many local shrines. Egyptian adepts were specially admired. Syria had probably many centres of psychic activity. Lucian wrote on 'The Syrian Goddess'. Much of all this came within the multifarious movement of 'Gnosticism', the movement of the 'Gnostics', which means 'those who know'. What they knew would be hard to say precisely. But it probably included the subject of 'Psychics'.

They maintained that they did not merely believe what they were told but had sure knowledge, themselves, of religious truth. They were freer than others to make their own investigations. Their beliefs could be most elaborately fantastic, and the whole subject is very complicated and difficult. But in part they were undoubtedly reacting to certain, perhaps many, kinds of psychic revelation.

What can surely be accepted is the fact that both Christians and Pagans were fully accustomed to paranormal phenomena; indeed the interventions from the other world were almost normal to many individuals and to some groups. Among the groups were the Pythagoreans and the Christians: among the individuals were Apollonius and St. Paul.

It has been said that the survival of the soul was just as well known before the Resurrection as after it, so that the great effect of Christianity cannot have been due merely to its promise of survival: Cicero in particular proving that this knowledge existed already. It is certainly true that the survival of the soul had been well known to very many people in many places for thousands of years before Christianity, and this is important. But the knowledge had mostly been either narrow and sometimes erroneous, or, as in Cicero, full of doubts and mystification. Cicero sometimes writes as if he is quite convinced and has a reasonable, if limited, system of knowledge, but at other times he will not go so far. Perhaps few went as far as Cicero at his time and place. There were, of course, different places: the ancient world was quite large. Perhaps a small, or even quite a large, minority of educated Romans believed in a future life. Perhaps, also, of the Jews in Palestine, only a few, and they perhaps on account of Greek influence, had any firm or coherent belief in it. The Sadducees said that there was no resurrection. This is, of course, before the first Easter Resurrection, so that, clearly, some did not believe in survival, and some did, before the evidence in which the New Testament culminates. That the soul survives was certainly not news to everyone either in the east or in the west of the ancient world in the years before the events of the Gospel narrative. But these events may still have corrected this knowledge, spread it, and made it valuable as never before.

There was, in the period covered by the New Testament, new and more plentiful evidence. And it was not confined to Christianity. Plutarch (*c.* A.D. 46–120), without saying much that is startling, shews a continuous interest in the probability or certainty that the soul survives. Apollonius of Tyana, who lived from about 4 B.C. to at least A.D. 100, and so exactly covers the New Testament period, was a famous Pythagorean philosopher who specialised in the psychic side of 'philosophy'. The long biography of him by Philostratus (*c.* A.D. 170–*c.* 244) is strung along a rich sequence of psychic events.[1] Apollonius was certainly a medium. He is reported to have achieved a number of exorcisms. That is, he cast out evil spirits. It might even appear, though any hasty comparison would be dangerous, that he cast them out exactly as they are cast out in the Gospels. Nor is it implied in the Gospels that exorcism there is new or different from what had been done before: 'If I by Beelzebub cast out devils, by whom do your sons cast them out?' (Matthew XII, 27).[2] There are plenty of parallels for exorcism in various parts of the world. But not much is heard of it in Greek and Roman antiquity till the first century A.D. Before then, the great healers and prophets certainly performed this service, but it may often be concealed by the verb *kathairein*, 'to purify', which is very widely used. Exorcism, both in the Gospels and the *Life of Apollonius*, is performed by rebuking the possessing (permanently) or obsessing (in attempted permanence) spirit. Normally, Apollonius speaks to them threateningly. Once he shewed a written document. The spirit always left the person afflicted, immediately, or soon. Ecclesiastical exorcism seems still to work in this way. But another kind is also in use at the present time. A medium reasons with the spirit, who is normally a former human being who is earth-bound and in need of enlightenment. The medium persuades him to recognise his condition and accept

K

the new life in the other world which is offered to him if he consents to it (see II, note 2, p. 181 below, on Dowding and Wickland, 'rescue circles'). This method is better, for the spirit then goes off happily and does no more harm. By the ancient, and the ecclesiastical, method he is ousted, but remains earthbound and will beset someone else, or perhaps an animal, such as the Gadarene swine. Exorcism is an example, one of the rare examples, of modern progress in the approach to the occult. We seem to have useful knowledge not open to the ancients.

Apollonius was credited with immense abilities. He detected and routed a disguised vampire who was planning to marry, and then devour, a young man. He could foretell the future, for example, shipwreck. He knew, though hundreds of miles away, the exact time when the Emperor Domitian was assassinated (Dio Cassius, 67, 18; Philostratus, *Vita Apollonii* VIII, 26). He transported himself, instantaneously and invisibly, from Rome to Dicaearchia, the modern Pozzuoli; and once also from Smyrna to Ephesus (*Vita Apollonii* VIII, 10; IV, 10). He controlled spirits, to exorcise them and otherwise: at his command a spirit knocked over a statue. He is credited with a kind of séance almost in a modern style. Being near the grave of Achilles in the Troad, and, unlike those with him, unafraid—he knew Achilles well, he said—Apollonius approached. He summoned the spirit of Achilles, and it arose out of the tomb and talked. Achilles had two complaints. Apollonius had with him a descendant of Achilles' enemy, King Priam of Troy: he must dismiss him— which, afterwards, Apollonius did. The second complaint was against the countrymen of Achilles in Thessaly. They had stopped sacrificing to him. They must start again, or he would make them pay, grievously. Apollonius took the message, and it was obeyed. If Apollonius was, as he has been called, 'the last word that Pagan Antiquity had to offer', he and his associates certainly fall far behind early Christian charity.

But Apollonius was a very strict moralist, and a puritanical religious zealot. He sacrificed at sunrise and midday to the sun. He sacrificed no kind of animal, but only spices, going as far, once, as a model of a bull made of spice, but no farther (*Vita Apollonii* v, 25). He would not even wear leather: his clothes were of linen and his shoes of biblus-fibre (*Vita Apollonii* VIII, 7). He was fiercely ascetic. He adopted Pythagorean philosophy when fifteen, and, though good-looking and liked by all, he repelled all intimacies, and lived in full austerity. He fits Ovid's description of Pythagoreanism as far as it goes. He knew his own previous incarnations, and sometimes the previous incarnations of others. He was not like a Buddhist: he put no full emphasis on loving kindness to all life. He did believe in gods, apparently the established gods of Greece, but perhaps in purified versions; he reorganised, and simplified, the worship at several temples. He denounced baths; but once he is said to have had one. He knew all languages; but once, in India, he needed an interpreter.

His command of the material world was particularly shewn at his arraignments, first before Tigellinus, the wicked minister of Nero, and later before Domitian, at Rome. He soon forced Tigellinus to dismiss him. His meeting with Domitian is a more elaborate story. He defended himself powerfully, broke the Emperor's confidence, and then vanished, to reappear almost immediately among his friends at Dicaearchia (*Vita Apollonii* VIII, 10). In prison, earlier, he had shewed his friends how he could escape. He simply withdrew a leg from its fetter, and then replaced it (Philostratus, *Treatise of Eusebius* XXXIV–XXXV).

Philostratus has very much more to report of Apollonius. Some of it is fanciful or legendary,[3] but much is likely to be sound: in matters in which he can be checked, as in the historical events mentioned, Philostratus seems to be accurate.[4] But perhaps further details, here, should wait for two other, and more urgent, considerations; Apollonius' relation with Christianity and to Neoplatonism.

In this period, as no doubt in others, there was a kind of change in the psychic balance. It is hardly to be explained; it just happened. It had different sides to it. There was a popular religious side. There was in the Roman West a passion for a personal, direct, contact with divine protectors, a demand for new, unofficial cults such as the cult of the composite deity Serapis and a newly understood Hermes. Presently the at first Indian, and then Persian, Mithras became immensely important. His religion, like many others, involved an initiation with salvation for the initiated. There came to be more fortune-telling, and probably more magic and more superstition. There was a great demand for such satisfactions and such services. Many shrines in many places grew in renown as they satisfied the demand. No doubt their priests made a good profit. Whether many of them cheated, or pretended to be more adept than they were, is not known. Some did; but no doubt many did not. There were elaborately fanciful rites, with mixtures of magic, witchcraft, and sorcery. But there was also a great deal of seriously argued and responsibly believed theology, especially Gnostic, associated with the religions. And initiates might often feel uplifted to a purer state, above the stress and degradation of the earthly world, as Apuleius felt. Lucian's attacks tend to prove not only that there were charlatans but that a great deal of honest occult practice was going on.

Much of all this may not concern the condition of the dead and beliefs concerning them. To the ancients, as to people in the Middle Ages, not all spirits were spirits of deceased human beings: only some were. 'Demonologies' described and distinguished the varieties and their status. There were demonologies before the ancient Greeks, in Babylonia and China. In late Egyptian magical papyri of the early Christian centuries a great number of names occur, more and more fantastic and grotesque, supposed to belong to deities or spirits who are to be conjured or mollified. Possibly someone placed these versions of 'the foul fiend Flibbertigibbet' in a hierarchy. Perhaps not many people seriously believed that all these names represented truly existing spirits, to be classified like Milton's 'Thrones, Dominations, Princedoms, Virtues, Powers'; or like the kinds of spirit which Iamblichus, the expert (probably *c.* A.D. 250–*c.* 325), could distinguish at his séances.

18 *Christianity*

It is strange, but it is also obvious and important, to reflect that this quaint, extravagant world is contemporary with the New Testament, or even overlaps with it.

The Old Testament often mentions the appearance of spirits. They are often called 'angels' in the translations, but they could be called 'communicators' without inaccuracy. Angels met and spoke to Abraham. Saul spoke to the spirit of Samuel through the medium, who was not necessarily in any bad sense a 'witch', as she has so often been called, at Endor (I Samuel XXVIII, 3–25).[1] The prophets, at least some of them at some times, prophesied under the control of spirits who spoke through them. Frequently, established or other authority disagrees with what spirits say. So, among the Hebrews, communication with the departed, though at times it flourished, was sometimes denounced. In such disagreements it is usually possible and sometimes necessary to sympathise with both sides. Neither living men nor departed spirits are always particularly good, or wise, or right in their opinions. But, though sometimes there seems nothing else to do, it is normally unwise to exclude altogether any source of information, especially a source capable of providing very much information, some of it highly authoritative.

Such was freely given by Jesus the Christ; and the Pharisees, and also the Sadducees who said that there was no resurrection, sought to suppress him, and his disciples, and his truth. The Roman provincial government could hardly help sympathising, on the whole, with the Jewish authorities, which it hardly liked, but must have thought safer. It must have been quite difficult for those who heard indirectly of Christianity even to suspect that there was any good in it fit to be taken seriously.

This time, however, the psychic contacts and communications were not trivial, and not misleading, but came from the Highest. Those who were close to the Master could hardly doubt even without any signs and wonders, but the signs and wonders were there. They were not miracles, but the exertion of power according to the laws of spirit and matter, a power so enormous that nothing else like it has ever been known, but still a power according with law. There is an acknowledgement of a heavenly world, in which the spirits of earthly dead survive, especially in the Transfiguration (Matthew XVII, 1–13; Mark IX, 2–10; Luke IX, 28–36), when spirits are seen. But the source of the power in a spirit-world can be, and has been, partly overlooked. The phenomena recorded in the New Testament, the Gospels and elsewhere, perhaps with the exception of certain things in Revelation, all belong to the psychic area of experience, the active borderland between the earthly-living and the departed. The borderland, however, can be conceived as the boundary between the human and the divine, between man and Almighty God.[2]

Early Christians were on the whole spiritualists. St. Paul wanted them to be: 'Concerning spiritual (i.e. psychic) gifts', he says, 'I would not have you ignorant'. Different gifts are allotted to different people: to one 'prophecy', or inspired speech; to another 'distinguishing of spirits'; to another 'tongues' (that is, giving messages in unknown languages); to another 'the interpretation of tongues' (I Corinthians XII, 7–11). St. Paul understood this important matter as Iamblichus two centuries later understood it. He, and the author of the First Epistle of St. John, are principally concerned to know whether each spirit is 'of God'. 'Test the spirits', we are told, the test being whether they acknowledge the divinity of Christ (John, Epistle I, IV, 1; cf. I Corinthians XII, 3. See p. 199 below, note 12); a question of momentous, or even appalling, importance today. Those who did not acknowledge the divinity of Christ were to be rejected. Those who did might aid in worship or in life.

St. Paul has at one point left us an interesting caution in regard to women attending Christian services. He says that they should not be bare-headed in church 'because of the angels' (I Corinthians XI, 10). In the Bible 'angel', the Greek word '*angelos*', 'messenger', can normally be translated as 'spirit', and may often mean the spirit of a deceased human being. St. Paul, by himself, is mysterious: the passage has caused considerable difficulty. Tertullian (*De Virginibus Velandis*, 7) takes him to be referring to bad angels either likely to become sexually tempted or to tempt men. But according to some of the early Fathers the Holy Ghost entered the Virgin Mary through her ears, and it has been suggested by Dr. Conybeare that a similar thought may lie behind St. Paul's passage.[3] According to this interpretation St. Paul wants some protection to be worn by women to guard their ears and prevent spirits from exercising an unauthorised control.

It has been said that the primary difference between two sorts of religion is the choice between the resurrection of the body and the survival of the soul and spirit. The nearly universal human belief is in the survival of the soul and spirit. Christianity now accepts, as did old Persian religions, the resurrection of the body.[4] Here St. Paul may be contrasted with Christian orthodoxy. He charges those who believe in a physical resurrection with folly. Instead, we leave, he says, our earthly bodies behind us, and survive in 'celestial' or 'spiritual', not 'terrestrial', bodies (I Corinthians XV, 40–4). He tries, it is true, to blend this doctrine with the other belief of resurrection:

We shall not all sleep, but we shall all be changed, in a moment, in the twinkling of an eye, at the last trump; for the trumpet shall sound, and the dead shall be raised incorruptible, and we shall be changed. For this corruptible must put on incorruption and this mortal must put on immortality.

(I Corinthians XV, 51–3)

'At the last trump' has been explained as a kind of Last Post
such as that sounded among the Jews at the end of the day and
also at the end of an individual's life to announce his passing.[5]
The suggestion then is, that it represents an individual's, rather
than a communal, transition. Though the New Testament
clearly associates the trumpet with simultaneous group resurrec-
tions for the Last Judgement (e.g., Matthew XXIV, 31; I Thessa-
lonians IV, 13-17; Revelation XI, 15), it can also sound in the
Old Testament as a more general symbol of the numinous,
accompanying God's terrifying manifestation to Moses (Hebrews XII, 19; Exodus XIX, 14-17). Trumpet sounds were widely
used in Hebrew religious ritual. The belief in the trumpet of
the Last Day, which St. Paul expected in the near future, may
accordingly be regarded as a natural extension of other trum-
petings, including those used for an individual's death. He seems
to be trying to adjust his intuition of an instantaneous change
('twinkling of an eye') at the approaching Last Day to the thought-
forms of a different tradition. The truth seems to be that we
do not wait. We are alive and active in our spiritual bodies as
soon as we pass over. Plato, and many today, would assert
that judgement directly follows decease. This is the teaching
of Christ himself, as expressed in his words from the cross to
the repentant criminal: 'Verily I say unto thee, To-day shalt
thou be with me in Paradise' (Luke XXIII, 43).[6]

However different, however special, the Biblical material
may be, it is at least true that in New Testament times there was
great psychic activity. Everything in the New Testament that
is apparently miraculous is said to have a parallel in secular
records. In India, for example, a man has walked on the water
without sinking. Even at Pentecost the occurrences are not
unique, but at least the power and concentration must be rare,
if no more. The tongues of flame seen on each head have their
correspondences in modern experience.[7] Inspired speech in
languages unknown to the speaker but understood by hearers is
familiar; it is called 'xenoglossy'. The rushing mighty wind is
not unique either: at the séance in *Gilgamesh* the spirit of Enkidu

appeared 'like a wind-puff'(Tablet XII, 84; see p. 33 above, note 1).[8]
The inspired condition of the Apostles is not to be explained—
the suggestion has been made—as a phenomenon like the emotional enthusiasm of Welsh oratory called 'Hwyl'. It is psychic.
St. Paul was peculiarly abreast with phenomena and theoretical
description. There is more waiting to be discovered about his
sources of information. He was a medium himself. Of one
experience he says (II Corinthians XII, 2, 3) that he had it 'whether
in the body or apart from the body, I know not': he may or may
not have been in trance at the time. This experience he had when
'in the third heaven'; reminding us of the Siberian shamans,
who claim to reach the sixteenth. But the merely psychic is
not all. The Vision on the Road to Damascus was rather truly
mystic than merely psychic.

The world of St. Paul is, in its mechanics, not unlike the world
of Apollonius of Tyana. Apollonius was, as we have seen, rapidly
transported from Rome after interviewing Domitian (p. 147
above). In the Acts of the Apostles, after he had converted the
Eunuch, 'the Spirit of the Lord caught away Philip', and he
'was found at Azotus', another rapid transportation (Acts VIII,
39–40). In both worlds possession by evil spirits is normal, and
exorcisms, of a similar sort, are practised. Human spirits can
occupy the bodies of animals: Apollonius met them in a lion
and a dog; and there are the Gadarene swine.[9] The stories may
not be true: in modern times a human spirit in an animal is,
to say the least, rare, though there is the recent wonder of 'the
talking mongoose of the Isle of Man'. What matters is that the
stories are similar.[10]

Even the Empty Tomb, at the Resurrection, might perhaps
be paralleled by the account of Machates' beloved, Philinnion,
who walked after death and left no mortal body in her grave:
but her mortal remains were found afterwards (p. 116–17 above). I
understand that no certain parallel to the Resurrection is known.
Philinnion's resurrection is not reliable enough to count as an
exception: her story has not the support of many well-attested
parallels and their cumulative persuasion. She may have returned,

even solid enough to embrace, but modern experiences of spirit-ualistic materialisations would support materialisation (p. 69 above) as the method, not any resurrection of the body. It is said that some Yogis in Tibet can achieve a temporary resurrection, reviving a dead body for ten or fifteen days. If so, there may be those who would classify the Resurrection in the Gospels with the Tibetan achievement. If not, agnostics might argue that since the story of Philinnion was altered, and they might add, perhaps by suggestion from necromancy (p. 69 above), then the Gospel story might have been altered too. A different, less likely, comment would allow the ancient world a wider psychic experience than the modern world, including a resur-rection of the body of a kind not recorded in recent centuries. In all these proposals a resurrection soon after death, and for a limited time, is posited.

There is a view that Christian doctrine was largely created or at least greatly changed when Constantine established Christ-ianity, and the Christian authorities adopted motives from Apollonius and elsewhere to enrich their message and recom-mend it to pagans. The Apocryphal Gospels may well have such additions, so added, but that is not to say that the Canonical Gospels are like them, though there certainly are interpo-lations in them, some very imaginative. It may be that such wonderful events were really happening at this time, and that they found their way into both Christian and pagan experience and books. It is not yet proved that criticism can harm the Gospel message.

Eusebius' most able answer to those who would exalt Apollo-nius and even rate him higher than Christ Himself is as important as it is fascinating. Writing about two centuries after Apollonius died, he asks why this notion had never been suggested until his time. Hitherto no one had thought of so exalting Apollonius, who had been regarded as nothing great, but as a wizard. Now a wizard, according to Eusebius, is one who compels spirits to do evil on earth for his own ends. This is just what Apollonius always denied. He was not a wizard. He was a philosopher. No doubt there might well be a possibility of mistake, an anxious matter. Apollonius certainly dominated spirits, but only for good ends. He himself was the judge of good and bad ends. Apollonius deserves trust and respect. But it was not easy for him to prove what was no doubt the truth, that his work was for good and not evil.

In a script dictated to a medium, Marjorie Livingston, and published in 1930 as '*The New Nuctemeron*'[11] with a preface by Sir Arthur Conan Doyle, a spirit calling himself Arcazaiel, aided by another called Zabdiel, presented a description of the world-process and the education and evolution of souls. The author at the conclusion of the script reveals that the professed name 'Arcazaiel' covers the historical name of Apollonius of Tyana. In his preface Sir Arthur Conan Doyle regards the document as a 'contribution to human knowledge' which 'is in all ways worthy of one of the greatest minds that ever functioned upon earth'. He says that it can 'stand or fall on its own internal evidence of authorship'. Repudiating 'vague talk of the subconscious self', he concludes: 'The book itself is its own best proof of a high external inspiration.'

Apollonius has become a Christian. This is not strange. The distinguished President of the Society for Psychical Research, the late G. N. M. Tyrrell, once observed that the higher Guides are all unreservedly Christian. This means that all the best, and most spiritual, spirits who communicate with and help people still living on earth acknowledge that Christ is Lord. There is still much dispute about the exact meaning to be attached to Tyrrell's statement, but its importance is in any case immense. One version, given at a séance by a very high Guide, should in particular be remembered: 'The Christ Spirit has always been in the universe. It was incarnate in the man Jesus. All the Guides call him "The Master".' St. John[12] demanded an assurance which is still freely given from the Other Side.

So Apollonius of Tyana, like Vergil, which is another story,[13] became a Christian after death. He accepts the divinity of Christ, but also sees him as crowning the achievements of pagan wisdom:

'We, on earth, were forerunners, proclaiming a Master Who was Nameless and Unknown, you are the followers of a divine Leader . . .' (*The New Nuctemeron* 32). But Christianity should not ignore the experiences that preceded:

It is not the Teachers of new revelations who have so trampled upon the labours of their predecessors, it is the fanaticism of their disciples that has suffered no commingling of doctrines. The Christ Himself destroyed nothing except the perverted interpretations of man.

Hence the modern world, living professedly in the Light of the World, has systematically ignored the fund of wisdom which was already known to the earth in the days of the Christ. He did not need to teach the philosophy of the Ancients; it was already accepted fact.

Therefore, amid the stimulus of transcendent gain, Mankind voluntarily discarded much by which it would have profited. The Christ did not come, no lesser Teacher has come, to supersede existing light, but to add to the sum-total of its beam (13–14).

'The philosophy of Egypt is not lost, but slumbers' (16).

Arcazaiel, or Apollonius, is not entirely orthodox. He is more ready now than he was on earth to respect the rights of the physical body and its pleasures (29). He opens with the formula 'In the Name of the Father, of the Son, and of the Holy Spirit' (13), but for him the Holy Ghost is less an individual deity than all spiritual communication between God and Man. Though he believes in the Incarnation of the Son of God (51), he deplores any ecclesiastical attempt 'to dictate an exact law or an exact creed' (16). Christ's 'atonement' does not mean atonement for the sins of individuals, but rather atonement for the existence of sin, or evil, on the earth (33); a man's progress depends on his own efforts (32). It is not the sinner but Evil that suffers the 'second death' of the Book of Revelation (44):[14]

Nought but that which is wholly evil shall undergo the Second Death, of which wrote the Apostle John. Nought but that which is evil shall become inert or be destroyed. God is Life, therefore that which is of God shall endure.   (44)

Cosmic law, which may involve suffering, must be fulfilled, for man's own good, but 'God has no Vengeance' (70) and 'there are none eternally damned' (50). Evil itself depends on the divine vitality and 'a great spirit, strong, and beloved of God may for a while be misled into such perversions' because its very strength makes it adventurous (61-2). When man discovers the full potentialities of his own mind he will become a 'superman'; but it would be most dangerous were he to discover them 'in his present state' (37, 36; and see 45).[15]

The general teaching conforms to that of other such messages from the higher spheres: as on man's spiritual body, radiant in accord with the degree of his achievement; on interpenetrating planes, distinguished by rate of vibration; on colours beyond the span of earthly sense-perception; on the possibilities of astral travel in sleep; and, for spirits, the painfulness of descent into earth conditions. There is an especial concentration on the concrete and even chemical nature of realities normally thought of as abstract, with many references to electricity.[16] Or he may define, with precision, the relation of the one state to another:

The fundamental Spark of Life is conscious, but, so far as we know, it possesses no brain-cells through which it may express the intelligence which it has inherited from its divine Source. It is, moreover, by nature acquisitive, and in its progress into the realm of Matter it attracts to itself various atomic elementals through which it becomes enabled to function and develops for a fragment of animating Force into an entity or Ego.

Descent, therefore, is essential to its independent existence. At this point, the entity is without knowledge or experience, and is merely in the state that it will acquire selectively those elements by which it may function coherently and is capable of registering experience and profiting thereby.   (22-3)

The teaching is throughout amazingly comprehensive, and rises to passages of rhapsody weighted with Christian fervour.[17]

Perhaps what is most striking is its evident *authority*, as noted by Conan Doyle, together with Arcazaiel's poignant admission of inadequacy: 'I have not the habit of this work and am accus-

tomed to it less than yourself' (21). He finds it hard to 'compress
and tabulate' the higher wisdom so as to 'force' it 'into the un-
willing gullet of Earth' (65). That is why Zabdiel, who is more at
home with our modern world, sometimes takes over control,
saying: 'My lord has much wisdom and great learning, but I
would constrain him sometimes to give that which is ever
more acceptable to earth conditions' (79).

The teaching is both pagan and Christian. Or we might say
that the great principle of Incarnation, attributed by Christianity
to Christ, applies here to all. Central to *The New Nuctemeron* is
the doctrine of emanation and remanation, of souls coming
down from on high into matter and slowly ascending again
through many incarnations till they are capable of eternal bliss,
and attain it:

Each unit of mankind must complete the Cycle of Existence before he
can have fulfilled his destiny . . . The Ego comes in touch with the
forces of evil, with conscious emotion, with definite physical experience,
and it is here, at the point of the Cycle exactly opposite to the high
State from which he came, that his struggle commences—that stupendous struggle which shall eventually bring him back to the divine State,
carrying within him Intelligence, Free-Will, Personality, a capacity for
the whole gamut of emotion, the power to enjoy eternal beatitude.

(24)

The doctrine is inherited from Pre-Socratic Greek philosophers,
and may be derived ultimately from India.[18]

Apollonius was in touch with the Beyond during his life on
earth, but he is not known to have learnt on earth the cosmology which he learnt, and revealed, after death. He was
unlike Plato's Er (p. 92 above), and the anonymous subject
of the experiment described by Clearchus, who after astral
travel returned and 'reported each thing' (p. 94 above and note 3).
But the tradition of this cosmology, of this descent of souls
into matter and their reascent, has a unity and a continuity
which are impressive. If regarded closely but also broadly,
it tends to seem like the truth.

19 *Neoplatonists*

The Christian representatives who 'formed a Government' of the Church for Constantine were on the side of the priests not the prophets. I believe that these are sharply distinguished in Biblical narrative and even in the Hebrew language. It is usual. It can often, too, lead to sharp conflict. It is easy to sympathise with both sides in this tragic dilemma. It is not always easy to 'test the spirits', or agree on how to judge them. To some it seems that Christianity was impoverished when this source of life and truth was dammed. It had been different earlier; it might have continued so, but for what looks like the accident of fourth-century history.

There seems to have been a psychic ferment during the first few Christian centuries. Possession, clairvoyance, and other such psychic experiences were widely taken for granted.

Especially important in this respect was the movement started in Phrygia by Montanus in the second century, which caused a schism within the Church. It developed a ministry of its own, which included women, and its prophets and prophetesses claimed a spiritual authority beyond that of the bishops and priests. 'Its prophesyings', writes Norman J. Bull, 'had great appeal at a time when the sense of the Spirit, as a living voice and power at work in the Church, was growing dim.'[1] It reached Rome, and then North Africa, where it won the acceptance of the great Tertullian about the year 200. Tertullian's *De Anima* contains an interesting passage on mediumship:

We have now amongst us a sister whose lot it has been to be favoured with sundry gifts of revelation, which she experiences in the Spirit by ecstatic vision amidst the sacred rites of the Lord's Day in church. She converses with angels, and sometimes even with the Lord; she both sees and hears mysterious communications: some men's hearts she understands, and for those who are in need she obtains directions for healing. Whether it be during the reading of the Scriptures, or the chanting of psalms, or the preaching of sermons, or the offering up of prayers, all these provide material for her visions.

If we have delivered some discourse on the soul while this sister of ours is rapt in the Spirit, then, after the people are dismissed at the conclusion of the sacred service, she is in the regular habit of reporting to us whatever things she may have seen in vision (for all her communications are examined with the most scrupulous care, in order that their truth may be probed). 'Amongst other things,' says she, 'there has been shewn to me a soul in bodily shape, and a spirit has been in the habit of appearing to me; not, however, a void and empty illusion, but such as would offer itself even to be held, soft and transparent and of an ethereal colour, and in form resembling that of a human being in every respect.' This was her vision, and for her witness there was God; and we have the authority of the apostle Paul that there were to be 'spiritual gifts' in the Church.

(*De Anima* 9, 4; adapted from the translation by P. Holmes)

Tertullian clearly accepted such contacts as an important element in Christianity.[2]

Psychic experiences sometimes came within Christianity and sometimes did not. The brief but revealing account in *The Acts of the Apostles* (VIII, 9–24) of the thaumaturge, Simon Magus, dramatises neatly what might be called a border-line case, and contrast. There are the comparatively well-known Apocryphal texts, *The Shepherd* of Hermas, *The Book of Tobit*, the books of Esdras, and perhaps above all *The Teaching of the Twelve Apostles* known as the '*Didachē*', 'Teaching', a genuinely psychic document. There was a culmination in the second century A.D., the time of Tertullian who supported psychic communication, and Lucian who mocked it, and found a great quantity of it to mock.

No doubt Lucian had met it before he left his early home in Syria. It may be guessed that from Egypt to Cappadocia there were to be found many 'prophets' or rather mediums, and also many shrines dedicated to a variety of gods, many of them small and little known, which relied on the practice of psychic abilities, as indeed to some extent Delphi did. Some of these operations and these centres of operation were respectable, and some not respectable, as happens today. Associated with some were the most extraordinary magical rites, or the most fantastic proliferation of divinities and divine names. Yet there was an underlying truth, and this truth was calmly accepted, and obeyed, by men who were scholars and saints. After all, in the age of the great Neoplatonists '*theourgos*', meaning a practising spiritualist, was a synonym for 'philosopher'.

Neoplatonism was successful and had many adherents. It accepted most of Plato's spiritual philosophy, and in addition to it the habit of consulting spirits through mediums. The thinking is almost painfully fine-drawn. The doctrine of the soul's destiny continues the tradition of Empedocles, Pythagoras and Plato.

In his *Essays: Classical* (London 1883 etc., 71–2) F. W. H. Myers writes:

We must go back as far as Hesiod to understand the Neoplatonists. For it is in Hesiod's celebrated story of the Ages of the World that we find the first Greek conception, obscure though its details be, of a hierarchy of spiritual beings who fill the unseen world, and can discern and influence our own. The souls of heroes, he says, become happy spirits who dwell aloof from our sorrow; the souls of men of the golden age become good and guardian spirits, who flit over the earth and watch the just and unjust deeds of men; and the souls of men of the silver age become an inferior class of spirits, themselves mortal, yet deserving honour from mankind.[3] The same strain of thought appears in Thales, who defines demons as spiritual existences, heroes, as the souls of men separated from the body. Pythagoras held much the same view and, as we shall see below, believed that in a certain sense these spirits were occasionally to be seen or felt. Heraclitus held 'that all things were full of souls and spirits', and Empedocles has described in lines of startling power the wanderings through the universe of a lost and homeless soul. Lastly Plato in the *Epinomis* brings these theories into direct connection

L

with our subject [Greek oracles] by asserting that some of these spirits can read the minds of living men, and are still liable to be grieved by our wrongdoing, while many of them appear to us in sleep by visions, and are made known by voices and oracles, in our health or sickness, and are about us at our dying hour. Some are even visible occasionally in waking reality, and then again disappear, and cause perplexity by their obscure self-manifestation.[4]

Myers was a great pioneer in applying modern psychic know-ledge to the elucidation of Greek antiquity.

Pythagoras himself (p. 76 above) is shadowy, but there are signs that he, no less than his followers, believed in the soul's survival, reincarnation, and indeed transmigration into, and also from, animal or vegetable forms of physical life. It is likely enough that he communicated with the dead, but not certain. His interest in mathematics, and music, whether or not it went very far, is hardly to be doubted, any more than his asceticism in food, drink, and sex: he is reported to have been a strict monogamist. Such is the spirit, and such, even if not exactly these, are the tenets of the Neoplatonists. For them, the soul is to learn by self-control and self-denial, and rise to even greater purity and perfection till it comes near to the Divine—for Plotinus, at least, God is neuter, so that 'the Divine' is a better expression than 'God'—and lives eternally in ecstatic contemplation of the universal order of all creation, the stars never varying from their courses, and the faultless and intricate mathematical structure of the world. Neoplatonists to some extent depended on mysticism, perhaps the first sure occurrence of it among the ancient Greeks and Romans: there may have been some earlier but it is hard to be sure whether the sublime experiences which are here and there described are of mystical or of merely poetical origin. Plotinus was certainly an ascetic, a saint, and a mystic. He was also a spiritualist, as were almost all pagan philosophers of his epoch.

The word for spiritualist was '*theourgos*', 'one who works at gods', or 'one who deals in spirits'. Communication through a medium was called '*theourgia*', 'divine operation'. The consultant was the 'operator', *theourgos*, and the medium the *docheus*, 'receiver'.

As we have seen, the word '*theourgos*' became practically synonymous with 'philosopher'. To be a 'philosopher' at all was at this time, in the second and third centuries A.D., to be a *theourgos*, so close had experimental spiritualism come to Platonic spiritual philosophy. It may seem slightly odd to find Greek philosophers, presumed to be tough intellectualists, being actually differentiated from other people by a word implying an occult basis for their activities. But we should remember that the greater Neoplatonists were not strictly Greeks by descent: neither Plotinus nor Porphyry was. They may have brought occult tendencies from their Asiatic homes.

Oracles gave answers more clearly than ever through controlled mediums, at Delphi and elsewhere. One of the greatest documents of the period, or indeed of all antiquity, is the answer of the Delphic oracle to Porphyry's friend Amelius when he had asked where the soul of Plotinus, the greatest of the Neoplatonists, had gone after his death. It is poetry, and it is revelation; the imagery gives colour and strength to the airy life now lived by the master in the holy place of the Highest. Here it is, translated by Myers (98–100):

> Pure spirit—once a man—pure spirits now
> Greet thee rejoicing, and of these art thou;
> Not vainly was thy whole soul alway bent
> With one same battle and one the same intent
> Through eddying cloud and earth's bewildering roar
> To win her bright way to that stainless shore.
> Ay, 'mid the salt spume of this troublous sea,
> This death in life, this sick perplexity,
> Oft on thy struggle through the obscure unrest
> A revelation opened from the Blest—
> Showed close at hand the goal thy hope would win,
> Heaven's kingdom round thee and thy God within.
> So sure a help the eternal Guardians gave,
> From life's confusion so were strong to save,

Upheld thy wandering steps that sought the day
And set them steadfast on the heavenly way.
Nor quite even here on thy broad brows was shed
The sleep which shrouds the living, who are dead;
Once by God's grace was from thine eyes unfurled
This veil that screens the immense and whirling world,
Once, while the spheres around thee in music ran,
Was very Beauty manifest to man;—
Ah, once to have seen her, once to have known her there,
For speech too sweet, for earth too heavenly fair!
But now the tomb where long thy soul had lain
Bursts, and thy tabernacle is rent in twain;
Now from about thee, in thy new home above,
Has perished all but life, and all but love,—
And on all lives and on all loves outpoured
Free grace and full, a Spirit from the Lord,
High in that heaven where windless vaults enfold
Just men made perfect, and an age all gold.
Thine own Pythagoras is with thee there,
And sacred Plato in that sacred air,
And whoso followed, and all high hearts that knew
In death's despite what deathless Love can do.
To God's right hand they have scaled the starry way—
Pure spirits these, thy spirit pure as they.
Ah saint! how many and many an anguish past,
To how fair haven art thou come at last!
On thy meek head what Powers their blessing pour,
Filled full with life, and rich for evermore!

'This', writes Myers, 'so far as we know, was the last utterance of the Pythian priestess'.

Behind the Neoplatonists there was the current and accepted operation of the séances. There was also the Pythagorean and Platonic tradition, seven or eight centuries of it. There was also the learning and wisdom of Alexandria and other great centres. And there was the Jewish contribution too, now plentifully canalised into the learned Pagan, as well as into the Christian, world. Here there were many currents. It is even possible that the religious feeling and moral ardour of Persia gave themselves both to the Jews of the later Old Testament and also to Socrates, to be handed down by him to all Platonists, and Neoplatonists, who themselves furnished the original substratum of early Christian philosophy. Philo of Alexandria (*c.* 30 B.C.–A.D. 45) was read not only by Jews, nor were the numerous other Jews of Alexandria heard only by their own race. Hence came the God of Righteousness, a God to follow and obey at all costs, and eventually a God to love: a God with demands on men, who needed men; not a God with contempt for all but certain favourites— despite the instances of favouritism apparent in the Old Testament.

The consultation of mediums at this period was closely in line with the same practice today. One of the signs is the puzzling occurrence among the communicating spirits of meteorological names such as 'Sun' or 'Moon' (p. 166 below). It appears that such names are often taken by the departed, now as then. Much is learnt about these matters from Plotinus (A.D. 205–269), who seems to have been a clairvoyant and mystic, and from Porphyry (A.D. 232–*c.* 305), who was not. Something is learnt from Proclus (fifth century A.D.), and something from Plutarch (*c.* A.D. 46—after 120), whose great learning and common-sense did not prevent him from believing in an after-life. To Plutarch is owed the interesting information that a Delphic prophetess actually died after being prematurely forced into trance, a report which strongly suggests that the Delphic prophetesses were always, or at least often, true mediums (p. 67 above, note 3).

The Neoplatonists, Porphyry, Plotinus, Proclus, Iamblichus and the Emperor Julian (A.D. 332–363; ruled 361–3), accepted the facts of survival and communication. Iamblichus (A.D. *c.* 250–*c.* 325) seems to have been the great master of this communication. He was deeply religious and believed in a saintly life. His principal book is *On Mysteries*. Within his subject there comes, for him, the art of 'theurgy', the technical knowledge needed for rich, useful, and devout communication between the worlds. He explains how the spirits are invited and identified, and how they communicate, and how sometimes they can be seen entering a medium. He gives directions for séances, on the whole closely parallel to what is done now, though some details are strange to see and hard to explain.[5] However, that is a small point. In the main, we find a well-established practice which to many now seems quite familiar. As we have seen, there are conventional terms. A medium is a *docheus*, 'receiver'. Communicating spirits give fantastic and barbarous names. This is half-way or more to the frequent experience today with spirits giving names such as Sunshine, Moontrail, Starbeam, Burning Sand, Silver Birch, or Red Cloud. Another advance of Iamblichus is his 'distinguishing of spirits' (I Corinthians XII, 10). He distinguishes communicators by their rank: gods, angels, *daimones* and the human departed. The distinction is important and carries conviction; but the classes seem to be to some extent ahead of present-day knowledge. It is not like a traditional demonology on which possibly learning has worked, evolving away from direct experience of ghosts or spirits. It looks, instead, as if it is very near to such experience and even in direct contact with it.

Iamblichus affirms, and was possibly the first to state clearly, a spiritualistic principle of the first importance, that in these matters like attracts like, and that if one who received communication is visited by an inferior spirit, it is because he himself is inferior in attainment and virtue. Aware of the dangers of fraudulent spirits, he and his associates held careful and devout séances, and gathered knowledge from them scientifically.

Neoplatonism, then, had contact with both the low and the high sources of religious or at least other-worldly practices and experiences. But it remained Greek and to some extent abstract. For Plotinus, God is 'the Divine', 'it' rather than 'he'. Nor did he like the Christians with their very personal God. He believed in, and argued ably for, the soul's immortality. He had the very special advantage of being a true mystic. It is hard to find true mystics in antiquity. True mysticism is often difficult to identify. There may be much more of it among Christians than elsewhere. Pagan mysticism can normally be called something else, whatever in fact it is. However that may be, Plotinus' mysticism was genuine. He describes the mystic experience, lifted out of his body into a realm of supernal beauty, and attaining to union with the Divine (*Enneads* IV, 8, I). He had experienced the feelings of inexpressible delight which come to mystics, and, like other mystics, in his revelation of it to others he lacked the symbols needed to convey the ineffable truth. But he is a seer who has been to Heaven and, however imperfectly, can report what he sees.

The vision of Plotinus is in important contrast with the Book of Revelation, and the quantity of even more recondite and fiery apocalyptic literature which was current in or near Persia, and of which considerable portions are extant. It might be asked whether they, unlike the visions of Plotinus, are in the tradition of Plato's Er the Armenian (p. 92 above), who, left for dead on the battlefield, revived, and revealed the moral government of the world and its mechanism. One possible view is that both source and development are different, the apocalyptic tradition having perhaps been started by some paranormal insight, and then developed by the pictorial imaginations of men on earth, until material existed from which a selection could easily be adapted to a Christian purpose, but not a purpose belonging to the earliest Christianity. At least there is a Throne and a Judgement, and a personal God with personal angels and devils and beasts by the Throne. It all belongs east of Greece; it has a hint of the Byzantine Christ Pantokrator, the All Ruling. Apocalyptic literature, unlike Plato's myth of Er, has no reincarnation: it has Heaven or Hell after one life on earth.

The mystic vision is one thing, and the psychic experience of clairvoyance or astral projection is another. There is also, among Greeks as among other peoples, the imaginative construction of Utopias, or happy lands of past, or future, or far away, or never to be real. The Greeks made such word-pictures for themselves in poetry from Homer onwards, and when prose came into use they made more word-pictures in prose and for long continued to do so. Lucian's grotesque example is famous. It would be of great interest if this third class of imaginary paradises could be shewn to have a psychic origin, in the sense that paranormal faculties have communicated a knowledge of fact. This may be possible eventually.

Iamblichus writes on 'Mysteries'. An ancient 'Mystery' was a religious performance by a kind of secret society consisting only of those who had been formally admitted to membership because, morally or otherwise, they were qualified. The root of the word, *mu*, means 'shut'. What went on at the most important Mysteries was a secret so well guarded that there is no evidence that it was ever revealed, though some people were wrongly accused of revealing some of the secrets. In later times there were more 'Mysteries' and apparently they were joined more lightly, as people join a club, or more lightly still. There were Mysteries of Isis. The effect of the ritual on the members can be guessed, and indeed is sometimes indicated. Apuleius (born *c.* A.D. 123) found in the Mysteries of Isis a blissful relief of spirit (*Metamorphoses* XI, 24). Mysteries could give assurance of a happy immortality. The Orphic Mysteries did, and the Eleusinian may have: they seem to have been meant to promote the fertility of the earth and also the prosperity of the souls of men, here and hereafter. Probably all Mysteries, the old and few and the younger Mysteries which were many, had some thought of survival. Iamblichus makes it the central concern of what to him are Mysteries. After an obscure history of hundreds and perhaps thousands of years, the purpose and practice of the 'Mysteries' reached the simplicity of maturity.

The Emperor Julian the Apostate called Iamblichus the greatest of the philosophers, even greater than Plato. Julian was a spiritualist, in conflict with the Christian Church which had positively abandoned spiritualism only a generation or so before. The issue was intense, as it often has been, and may be again soon. What is contained in it is displayed in Ibsen's *Emperor and Galilean*. To the Emperor the Christianity known to him must have seemed coarse and unphilosophical.

How many individuals in the Mediterranean world of later antiquity practised communication, and had good hope, and some intelligible conception, of an after-life, cannot be guessed, but the number may be quite large. Lucian, roughly contemporary with Plotinus, ridicules many things, if not everything, in his gay and humane satiric dialogues, and he certainly thought that spiritualism was of sufficient public interest to be included. Many who enjoyed Lucian must yet have been themselves believers. Certainly Apollonius of Tyana had a great following who after his death looked forward to his second coming, as indeed some looked forward to Nero's (Suetonius, *Nero* 57). And indeed the vigorous hostility of the Christian Church, after the first two centuries or so, towards spiritualism proves that it was widespread enough to fear.

In this story St. Augustine holds a place of great importance. He lived late in the fourth and early in the fifth centuries A.D. He was born a pagan but his mother was a Christian. He went through phases of Manichaeism and Platonism, but was converted by his mother and wrote a criticism of pagan philosophy. He soon passionately loved the Old and New Testaments, and was content with them and his own numerous, long and powerful expositions of them. He was a philosopher of high quality and one of the ablest and most original psychologists known to history. To him Christianity was philosophically far superior to Platonism. He himself had some psychic powers and was perhaps occasionally clairvoyant. Among his acquaintances were more than one 'sensitive', and he carefully experimented with their abilities.[6] He did not think this wrong; but what happened had not much explicitly to do with communications between the worlds. His own outlook on the whole subject is interesting. He knew that there was something in it but preferred not to guess at explanations, and, if anyone else had any account to offer, he would much rather listen to him than make any contribution of his own (*De Genesi ad Litteram* XII, 18, 39; Migne 34, 469). It is strange that a former Platonist who was still to some extent a Platonist should seem so unaware of discoveries made by the Neoplatonism which gave to early Christianity its main philosophical sub-structure.

The Christian Hell, Purgatory, and Heaven were now established, and those who wondered what came after death could be told. Those who wished to enquire more exactly, an enquiry quite possible but involving difficulties and demanding besides moral qualities great accuracy and discrimination, were impeded. The Christian Other World was based on Scripture and also other traditions, for example Egyptian, though this may be denied, and Etruscan. It is on the whole static, not a world of high activity and progress. It is reached after a long sleep and the resurrection of the body after a Last Trump.

There is a modern view that the doctrine concerning the resurrection of the body is distinguished from doctrines concerning only the future life of the soul or spirit by a very important demarcation indeed. It is clear that confusion may arise between the physical body and the etheric or astral body known to clairvoyants. The distinction was difficult and confusion easy. Very many peoples, such as the ancient Egyptians and modern Tahitians and Yoruba, have carefully noted or worked out several parts in the personality or soul. They could have believed that the physical body is emphatically not the part that survives. Yet often, or even most often, this body has been treated as still very important after its death. Even the exceedingly well-informed Egyptians did this, apparently believing that the divine Pharaoh's soul, accepted by Amun-Re, yet depended on the preservation and safety of his mortal remains. Perhaps it was a matter of effective symbolism or magical sympathy. Greeks and Romans thought that rest in the beyond depended on formal, ritual burial. It has been hard for humanity, even advanced intellectual humanity, to doubt the value of ritual. Empedocles believed in it, Plotinus on the whole did not.

Plotinus, Porphyry and Iamblichus, to whom the Emperor Julian probably deserves to be added, furnish the achieved result of Greek and Roman experience and enquiry into the after-life. Theirs is a coherent account, based on well-observed facts, not least moral and spiritual facts. Many today would grant that they secured the most precious and important part of the truth as it now appears to them to be. They struggled to the right answer, as Aristarchus (*c.* 310–230 B.C.) found the right answer for the movements of sun, moon, and planets, but like him failed to found an accepted orthodoxy; and yet they managed well without the discoveries of physics which this subject really needs.

They were faced by a choice between apparent impossibilities, and chose well. They imagined souls existing in the air, in a hierarchy of planes or levels. They needed a theory to shew how worlds might interpenetrate because existence in one uses different atomic quanta from existence in the others. This seems to be the truth. It is not enough to think of souls as invisible in the air. They must be visible to someone, and indeed to each other. And so they may be, if they and their new world are understood as using their own different, but real, material constitution, and able to act on wavelengths detectable among themselves and sometimes even to some of those still living on the earth. In the world of the after-life there are many mansions, and many very different pictures of it may be equally true. It is certainly a rich, active and various world, with service to others still, and more than ever, and with a hope of eternal life and progress.

Some may argue that the Christian doctrine of the after-life is schematic, an outline near the truth but designed to be easy to teach and easy to keep the same without perilous fluctuations. Hell, Purgatory and Heaven are not exactly what exist; but the words express something like what does exist. It is also true that Heaven and Hell and also Purgatory are within us: they are not places but conditions of life and feeling. It is also possible to argue that the sleep till Judgement Day and the Last Trump are not exactly untrue but off-centre. Apparently we are judged, as Plato said, or judge ourselves, immediately after death, though there may be some who sleep first. We do not all wait till one Day of Judgement for all. As we have seen (p. 152 above), the Last Trump has even been explained as relating rather to an individual than to all men. Ancient Jews used to announce an individual's death by a note on a trumpet, so that people could stop work, and perhaps say a prayer. It was the trumpet used to call the flocks home in the evening, like the original Last Post.

20 The Church
Conclusion

And yet Christianity furnished what Paganism lacked. What exactly that was is not for me to say. But perhaps it was above all the personality and wisdom and universal love of the Master sent by God, reinforced by revelations concerning the life and destiny of every soul which were already foreshadowed in the pagan progress, to which the New Testament is sometimes nearer than it is to orthodoxy, but not always. The Kingdom of God is in the Spirit World; and it is like the Parables. They may be what matters most; and this world should follow them too, for God's Kingdom is to come on earth.

The two worlds, if they can be called two, are obviously to some extent interdependent. The other world is peopled from this. It can be changed from this, as it in turn can influence by its guidance, as Hesiod knew, this world of earth. And like attracts like. If the Egyptians knew a happy heaven with kind spirits, they helped to make it, and to provide, or attract, them. If Homeric Greeks or their predecessors in belief imagined a dreary Hades, perhaps they had faults which made this so, or qualities which attracted such weaker spirits into their view. If Pindar and Vergil augustly or lovingly pictured souls in bliss on the sunshine grassland, they may have been the right men to find this sight before their eyes or this imagination in their minds. If Empedocles and Plotinus and a Delphi, maturer now, could conceive a life near God where passion and strife were gone and only love remained, this may be due to their own gifts of the spirit.[1]

Meanwhile those who go from here take thoughts and memories and desires. Their self-denials are rewarded. They get what they have wished; their wishes help to make their new home; and what they have they share.

Accordingly the other world, or the parts of it to which those who die from the earth may go, may well have changed considerably. Our own hope of a happy future there, according to our plentiful evidence, is bright. And perhaps it is all the brighter for the lives lived here in antiquity by the great and good.

From the fourth century onwards the Greek Oracles were steadily suppressed by the State. During Julian's short reign, Delphi is said to have given its final answer, though the words came not through the mediumship of the priestess but mysteriously in a voice from no definable source: 'Tell the King: to the earth has fallen the glorious dwelling'. Nothing was left to the God Apollo. 'The water-springs that spake are quenched.'[2] Repressive measures continued. In short, the spirits, who long before, as the '*manes*', were not allowed to embarrass the pagan Roman Pontifices, were now not allowed to interfere with the Christian authorities, who like the Pontifices claimed the sole right to regulate relations between the earthly and the spiritual world; and were far more repressive, for Christians of the winning party persecuted their opponents as cruelly as they had been persecuted, or more.

At first the early Church had used mediums at their services. They depended on them for encouragement and advice and all the vital truth which can be gained from spirits who may be several stages nearer wisdom and perfection than men on earth. St. Paul spoke so emphatically on spiritual and psychic gifts, and the events recorded in the Acts of the Apostles, especially at the first Pentecost when the Holy Spirit came on the Disciples, were so clear in their implications, that Christians could hardly refuse to look through the veil, even if as through a glass, darkly.

There was, however, a possibility of controversy. Signs and

wonders had come very fast, and we cannot be sure that at the time the perspective was long enough. There was also a strong inclination to link present experience with traditions from the past, and to find a simpler formula than the wealth of new recognitions invited. It was possible to think more about the Holy Trinity and less about the spirit-world. But contact with the spirit-world was maintained, especially in the early centuries, the very times when pagans who knew Christians were forced to admire the unique holiness of life which made them happy and caused others to wonder at such inhuman, paradoxical behaviour as it seemed to them.

In the third and fourth centuries controversy quickened and tightened. St. Jerome, Origen and Eusebius considered Christian spiritualism and saw its disadvantages and dangers. When Constantine, who perhaps himself had some psychic sensitivity, accepted Christianity for Rome, he had helpers ready to establish an orthodoxy less dangerously fluid than the former freedom. Opinions differ on the question whether he was right. But all can agree that those responsible for church government must always find the possibility of perpetual interventions, some of which claim authority much higher than theirs, at least embarrassing, and sometimes even, from their point of view, a deadly menace to a true Faith. A St. Joan does not come every day, but might come at any time.

Not that in either the Western or Eastern Churches unusual powers and strange phenomena disappeared. They did not, and had usually to be accepted by authority. An intriguing psychic story is reported by Dr. A. P. Stanley, following the *Ecclesiastica Historia* (VIII, 23) of Nicephorus. Dr. Stanley is writing of the first Council of Nicaea:

Some singular legends adorn this stage of the proceedings. It was believed in later times that two of the three hundred and eighteen Bishops, Chrysanthus and Mysonius, who had entirely concurred in the views of the Council, had died before the close of its sessions, and been buried in the cemetery of Nicaea. When the day for the final subscription arrived, the Bishops took the volume to the grave of the two dead men, addressed them, as Mussulmans still address their dead saints, and solemnly conjured them, that, if now in the clearness of the Divine Presence they still approved, they would come and sign with their brethren the decrees of the Faith. They then sealed the volume, and laid it on the tomb, leaving blank spaces for the signatures, watched in prayer all night, and returned in the morning, when, on breaking the seal, they found the two subscriptions, 'We, Chrysanthus and Mysonius, fully concurring with the first Holy and Oecumenical Synod, although removed from earth, have signed the volume with our own hands.'[3]

What actually happened, if anything really happened, for our only authority for the legend is medieval, we cannot say; and it would probably be rash to speculate. Examples of spirit-writing independent of a human scribe have been reported in our own time.

Levitation is often mentioned, up to the example of St. Thomas Aquinas,[4] and after. Certain prophecies also were admissible, and even acts called miracles, which are in fact among the qualifications for sainthood in the Roman Church. Peculiar powers were readily accepted as signs of holiness, and sometimes they are that. But some powers counted as evil, and especially the power to communicate with familiar spirits. These powers were counted as witchcraft. In the Eastern Church, especially during the early centuries after the separation, there are many accounts of psychic gifts and acts; but they are within, not against, the ecclesiastical authority. St. Augustine, too, who thought about the persecution of heretics and came to approve of it, freely records the interesting, if not very exciting, psychic abilities, largely telepathic, of his acquaintances. When he himself received what he took to be a miraculous Divine command, hearing the words '*tolle lege*', 'take up (the Book) and read' (*Confessions* VIII, 29), he did not suspect that it might be an instance of 'psychic communication'.

Meanwhile the picture of the other world becomes fixed. There is Hell, Purgatory and Heaven; and they are well understood within the limits of doctrine. There could always be visions, and even messages between that world and this, but they were subject to control, and to seek messages was forbidden. The persecution of witches is thought to have restricted communication severely. But it did not stop it.

Wizards, witches, necromancers, and witch-doctors—or exorcists and healers who corrected the harm done by wizards and others—were of course among the persecuted, and so, with fluctuations, it continued to be: the last traces of persecution survived in Britain at least until the repeal in 1951 of the Witchcraft Act. But there have been fluctuations, and times, and places, at which no hurt came to the dissidents, including the psychically gifted.

The great wars of our own epoch have encouraged interest in spirit-communication. It may sometimes have been so in the past. The reassurance of Brownings's *Abt Vogler* that 'there shall never be one lost good', which is the lesson of spirit-communication, can be a great and precious consolation. There are alternatives, in traditional religion and in philosophy, including the contemplation of Nature and her splendid power, not to be overcome, in a world of which we are part. Such is *The Consolation of Philosophy* written out by Boethius, in person, awaiting execution by barbarous captors. This brave, sensitive, pathetic and generous work consoled at least one opponent of Mussolini during the last great war. It consists of many short passages, some in prose and some in verse, in which the Bible and also the Greek and Roman Classics are remembered, and used. The philosophy of man, and his poetry, supplement the Word of God. The other world for Boethius is a land from which no traveller returns. He never thinks of the precious confirmation of belief which human doubt so often seems to need.[5]

But a spirit-world exists, and has always existed, and all those who seem to die go to it. The existence of this world, and many facts concerning it, have now been proved beyond reasonable doubt, mainly through clairvoyance and mediumship, during the last century or a little more.

All the races of mankind, including the Greeks and Romans,

M

have known this world by direct experience, often recorded, if at all, as what we may well call 'folklore'. Civilisation tends to reduce psychic sensitivity, and it seems to have reduced it for a time among the Greeks and Romans. One of several reasons why it does so is the difficulty of reconciling the phenomena with intelligent thought, to which they may well seem impossible and their mythological expression fantastic. Accordingly the mind comes to reject sure fact because it is inexplicable. Some of the ancients, however, made great progress by what should be called scientific care allied to spiritual purity. Their results, which taken together amount to a coherent system of well-attested belief, agree impressively with modern psychic knowledge.

This modern knowledge is no longer repellent to reason since physical science is now able to show that psychic phenomena are in no way incompatible with the nature of the physical world. In view of these considerations a more sympathetic approach to records of the past, and some re-examination of them with a clearer perspective, appear to be required.

NOTES TO CHAPTER 1

1. (p. 25) In ancient Egypt the death and resurrection of Osiris applied first to 'the king's fate and not that of everyone'; 'only the kings and their favourites could become an Osiris after death'. Subsequently 'the scribal and military classes clamoured to share in the Osiris fate after death', and eventually the rites began to 'reflect the inward feelings of ordinary men and women' (R. T. Rundle Clark, *Myth and Symbol in Ancient Egypt*, London 1959, 124–5).

2. (p. 26) For a volcano as the home of the more favoured dead, see John Layard, *Stone Men of Malekula* (London 1942), 5, 226–33, 275–7, 532, 732. Those of high rank go to the volcano, those of lower rank into caves (231, 236–7, 276–7).

NOTES TO CHAPTER 2

1. (p. 33) Conditions are arranged for the appearance of Enkidu from the underworld: see Tablet XII, lines 77 ff. in *Ancient Near Eastern Texts etc.*, ed. James B. Pritchard (2nd ed. Princeton 1955), 98–9. Tablet XII, an appendage to the main epic, has a value of its own.

2. (p. 33) See pp. 63–4 above. Cf. also Rundle Clark (above, I, note 1), 120–1. Of the *Ka's*, i.e. the ancestral spirit-powers, Mr. Clark writes: 'Not the terrestrial residence, but the tomb, was the house of the *Ka* and the mortuary priest was the "servant of the *Ka*". These ideas seem inconsistent to modern minds, but the Egyptians were living very close to their collective past and held on to such primitive patterns of belief with great persistence. The living did not worship their ancestors, but hoped that some of the power which resided among the ancestors could be transmitted for their own needs. The tomb was for the living as much as for the dead.' Burial grounds were so planned that the dead could 'lie close together in a family or clan solidarity'; 'the desire to

lie close together, and to preserve for ever the ties of family affection, was the chief motive in the arrangement of the *mastabas* around the great pyramids. The private tombs were invocations to the living and the outer rooms were intended to be visited by the surviving members of the family, above all on New Year's Day when, more than at any other time, power flowed into the world from the source—not so much beyond as in the grave.'

The official, more 'generalised' god, Osiris, 'developed in this context, but transcends it', being 'a composite of royal theory and popular pressure'. The living King was 'Horus', the son of the deceased 'Osiris'. Osiris 'was the deceased monarch as well as the embodiment of fertility. He was not the ancestor in the old anonymous sense but the lord of the ancestors and unique inheritor of their power. As the old king he carried his royal function into the next world to become the Lord of the Dead, the president of a ghostly court. Osiris was both Hades and Dionysus.'

The living king was the 'mediator' between the community and the sources of divine power, either in the sky or from the ancestors. The relevance of these passages, in phrase after phrase, to the tenets and practice of Spiritualism in any period will be reasonably clear. The development from the spiritualistic to a communal and royalistic theology corresponds to the birth of Christianity from the soil of ancient occultism, in oracle and elsewhere.

There is another relevant passage, on the 'Coffin Texts'. The worship of Osiris as god developed, we are told, into a more 'personal' concern, reflecting 'the inward feelings of ordinary men and women', who wanted their loved ones to become an 'Osiris' in death, and so live (Clark, 125). At one point in the ritual, a voice is heard from the dead: 'The "call" of Osiris for help is the great turning-point in the drama. Apparently it was "Come down to me!", "*Ha-k ir-i*", which gave the name "Haker" to the great festival at Abydos. The old texts hint at the tension of this moment "when, during the night of the Great Sleep", the call of the god was heard outside by the worshippers. During this night no sound of music or singing was to be heard, for all were waiting for the moment when the god should cry for help. Also, in the ritual for "Opening the Mouth" the chief officiating priest pretended to sleep and dream that his (Horus') father had called out to him. He then rose to answer the call, and this was the beginning of the operative part of the ceremony. In the myth—and it is also implied in the ritual—Horus descends to the Underworld and there embraces his father and "recognises" him. That means, as we have seen, that Horus receives the *Ka* of Osiris' (130). For the 'Opening of the Mouth' see Clark, Index.

The attendant devotees would, presumably, be identifying themselves with Horus and their dead one or ones with Osiris. This dramatic ritual seems either to be, or to be deliberately re-enacting, experiences of clairaudience and trance-mediumship, with the priest as medium; and perhaps even of some kind of spiritualistic materialisation. The cry of the dead for help from the living has an obvious parallel in the beliefs activating the rituals and prayers reported in W. Y. Evans-Wentz's *The Tibetan Book of the Dead* (London 1927); and also in the rescue-circles of modern Spiritualism as described by Air Chief Marshal Lord Dowding in *Lychgate* (London 1945). See also Carl A. Wickland, *Thirty Years Among the Dead* (London 1947). For a description of Osiris' plight in 'a depth unfathomable' of darkness, without 'water' or 'air', see Clark, 139.

Since composing this note I am privileged to be able to quote a clear statement written for me by Mr. Rundle Clark: 'At Abydos there was a festival called "Haker": this means "Come down to me", presumably a cry for help. Both in the Haker ceremony itself and in the normal statue dedication ceremony the officiating priest crouched on the ground, pretending to be asleep. He was supposed to dream that his father Osiris called to him for help, Osiris being imagined as lying in a dark underground place, dead or helpless and suffering. The priest awakes as the son, Horus, and proceeds to bring offerings to the statue: this symbolised his coming to rescue his father. The actual "opening of the mouth" of the statue (Osiris) was the final and decisive act of restitution. This rite was certainly carried out for two and a half millennia. Osiris is the dead king, the dead man; Horus is the living king, the successor or heir. Each is indispensable to the other.'

Mr. Clark tells me that the Egyptians 'wrote letters to their dead, asking for advice or assistance in domestic crises'.

The statue is interesting. For the relation of statues in myth (the Don Juan myth) and literature (Shakespeare, Ibsen, Yeats, Shaw) to spiritualistic materialisations, see G. Wilson Knight, *Ibsen*, Writers and Critics Series (London and New York 1962), 102–3. The Pygmalion myth might also be adduced.

Probably the first to indicate the spiritualistic elements in the culture and practice of ancient Egypt was Gerald Massey, to the importance of whose work my attention has been drawn by Mr. D. Shaw, who is preparing a biographical account of his life and thought. Mr. Shaw sends me the following quotation from Massey's *Ancient Egypt* (London 1907), 150–4:

Spiritualism proper begins with the worship of ancestral spirits, the spirits of the departed, who demonstrate the continuity of existence hereafter by reappearing to the living in phenomenal apparition . . .

Herbert Spencer proclaims that 'the first traceable conception of a supernatural being is the *conception* of a ghost' (*Data*, 281) . . .

African Spiritualism, which might be voluminously illustrated, culminated in the Egyptian mysteries . . .

The Egyptians were profoundly well acquainted with those abnormal phenomena which are just re-emerging within the ken of modern science, and with the hypnotic, magnetic, narcotic, and anaesthetic means of inducing the conditions of trance. Their *rekhi* or wise men, the pure spirits in both worlds, are primarily those who could enter the life of trance or transform into the state of spirits, as is shown by the determinative of the name, the phoenix of spiritual transformation . . .

The persistence of the human soul in death and its transformation into a living and enduring spirit is a fundamental postulate of the Egyptian Ritual and of the religious mysteries. The burial of the mummy in the earth is coincident with the resurrection of the soul in Amenta, which is followed by its purifications and refinings into a spirit that may be finally made perfect . . .

It will suffice to show how profound the spiritualism must have been when the prayers and invocations are made, the oblations and the sacrifices are offered, not to the person of the deceased (who is represented by the dead mummy), but to the ka-image of his eternal soul, which was set up in the funeral chamber as the likeness of that other spiritual self to whose consciousness they made their religiously affectionate appeal. They make no mistake as to the locality of consciousness . . .

All ancestor worshippers have been spiritualists in the modern sense who had the evidence by practical demonstration that the so-called dead are still the living in a rarer, not less real form. The ancestral spirits they invoke and propitiate were once human, not the elemental or animistic forces of external nature, which under the name of spirits have been confused with them . . .

Massey gives a number of instances, quotations and references.

(G.W.K.)

3. (p. 35) For a comprehensive handling of the moral emphasis in ancient Egyptian belief and practice see James Henry Breasted, *The Dawn of Conscience* (New York 1933).

4. (p. 36) On 'shamans' and the Greeks, see E. R. Dodds, *The Greeks and the Irrational* (Berkeley 1951). A fascinating study of shamanism appears in J. D. P. Bolton, *Aristeas of Proconnesus* (Oxford 1962), which contains a comprehensive bibliography on the subject. See also Mircea Eliade,

Shamanism: Archaic Techniques of Ecstasy, trans. W. R. Trask (London 1964).

5. (p. 36) At Les Trois Frères there is a drawing of a 'sorcerer' in animal disguise: see G. R. Levy, *The Gate of Horn* (London 1948), 22, 23, 43, and Plate 2 (b).

6. (p. 37) The term 'astral' may be applied to out-of-the-body projection either on earth or within some new sphere. There are many relevant publications. See Robert Crookall, *The Study and Practice of Astral Projection* (London 1961), App. I 'History of the Subject', 145–59; also 'Acknowledgments', 229–31.

NOTES TO CHAPTER 3

1. (p. 41) *Ancient Near Eastern Texts*, ed. James B. Pritchard (2nd ed. Princeton 1955), 483–90.

2. (p. 42) T. B. L. Webster's authoritative interpretation appears in *From Mycenae to Homer* (London 1958), 35 ff., 41 f.

3. (p. 43) Sir Arthur Evans' arresting interpretation appears in *The Journal of Hellenic Studies* 45 (1925), 1–75, and in his *Palace of Minos* (London 1930) III, 145 ff.

4. (p. 43) There are others: see T. F. Royds, *Virgil and Isaiah* (Oxford 1918), App. C 'Messianic Passages in Isaiah'. For John Cowper Powys' life-long concentration on a *past* Golden Age, see G. Wilson Knight, *The Saturnian Quest* (London 1964).

5. (p. 43) Genesis V, 24. See also Hebrews XI, 5: 'By faith Enoch was taken up so that he should not see death; and he was not found, because God had taken him.'

6. (p. 44) On burial and cremation, see H. L. Lorimer, 'Pulvis et umbra' in *The Journal of Hellenic Studies* 53 (1933), 161–80; also now Vassos Karageorghis, *Salamis in Cyprus* (London 1969).

NOTES TO CHAPTER 4

1. (p. 47) We might compare Mao Tse-tung's recent exhibition of long-distance swimming, done for a similar purpose.

2. (p. 47) W. J. Woodhouse, *The Composition of Homer's Odyssey* (Oxford 1930) VII.

3. (p. 49) This theme is treated in greater detail in W. F. Jackson Knight, *Vergil: Epic and Anthropology*, ed. John D. Christie (London 1967), Part Two 'Cumaean Gates'.

4. (p. 49) J. Rendel Harris, *Scylla and Charybdis* (Manchester 1925), 24–5, citing Bérard; Cyrus H. Gordon, *Before the Bible* (London 1962), 269, where there is an interesting discussion on *ereb* and parallels meaning 'west' in Hebrew, Ugaritic and Akkadian.

5. (p. 49) Vittorio D. Macchioro, *Classical Philology* 23 (1928), 239–49. Cf. Denys Page, *The Homeric Odyssey* (Oxford 1955), 48 note 3, for other relevant references.

6. (p. 50) See p. 48 above. Heracles is, however, met also in Hades. In *Vergil: Epic and Anthropology* (above, note 3), 148, Jackson Knight wrote: 'In the *Odyssey*, Heracles is met in the world below; but Homer adds, in words that have been thought an interpolation, "only his ghost; for he himself had gone to Heaven" (*Od.* XI, 601–4)'. In 'The After-Life in Greek and Roman Antiquity', *Folklore* 69 (1958), 224, he wrote: 'Heracles, as Miss G. R. Levy explained, has in fact two lives, and there is no need to alter the text.' He cites G. Rachel Levy, *The Journal of Hellenic Studies* 54 (1934), 40–53. Elsewhere (*Vergil: Epic and Anthropology*, 145) he cites W. J. Perry, *The Children of the Sun* (London 1923), 255, on the beliefs of certain Pacific tribes: 'Their ghosts go underground, but the "life" of a dead man goes to the sky.'

Homer's lines on Heracles appear, as has already been observed by Edward Carpenter, *The Drama of Love and Death* (London 1912), 265, note, to be handling what may be a distinction of general import for spiritualistic studies. Cf. p. 62 below.

7. (p. 52) From Jackson Knight's use of the same material in his essay, 'The After-Life . . . ' (above, note 6) it seems that the statement refers to the Masai.

8. (p. 52) In making this point in his essay, 'The After-Life . . .' (above, note 6), 228, Jackson Knight has a footnote: 'I gratefully thank Dr. G. B. Gardner for recalling to me in conversation his own experience in

Borneo, where the living and the "dead" enjoy a daily intercourse with much advice from the "dead" on practical affairs.'

9. (p. 52) President Kenyatta has, however, recently made a vigorous attack on the grosser kinds of superstition involving the slaughtering of black goats and chickens in the belief that they bring ill luck. See *The Times*, 17 January 1968 (*In Brief*, 'Kenyatta hits at witchcraft').

10. (p. 53) The release of Tityos by Rhadamanthus is imagined in John Cowper Powys' *Morwyn* IV, 270–1: see G. Wilson Knight, *The Saturnian Quest* (London 1964), 66.

11. (p. 54) F. W. H. Myers, *Essays: Classical* (London 1883 etc.), 71; Erwin Rohde, *Psyche: the Cult of Souls and the Belief in Immortality among the Greeks*, trans. W. B. Hillis (London 1925), 67–79.

12. (p. 54) In 'The After-Life . . .' (above, note 6), 225–6, Jackson Knight cited Charles Autran as follows: 'Hesiod's Golden Age is apparently Asiatic. Autran, in an unpublished manuscript which I am allowed to mention now, traces it to very ancient Asiatic beliefs in which a dethroned high god, an Asiatic Cronos, lived and reigned over the older heroes in a golden land under the earth. That Hesiod used Asiatic sources for some myths had already been shown, especially by Ludolf Malten.'

13. (p. 55) Rohde (above, note 11), 71.

14. (p. 55) See the section on Homer (26–34) in Mrs. St. Clair Stobart's *The Either-Or of Spiritualism* (London 1928), discussed on p. 12 above.

15. (p. 55) Fernand Robert, *Homère* (Paris 1950), 1–62.

16. (p. 55) Compare the telepathic action of helping spirits in John Masefield's *Right Royal*. It is fascinating to watch a modern poet in the Homeric tradition giving that tradition a spiritualistic interpretation.

17. (p. 56) It may be worth observing that the heroes of both the *Iliad* and the *Aeneid*, Achilles and Aeneas, are helped by divinities, Thetis and Venus, who are also their mothers.

NOTES TO CHAPTER 5

1. (p. 57) Maria Helena Monteiro da Rocha-Pereira, *Concepções Helénicas de Felicidade no Além de Homero a Platão* (Coimbra 1955). See also Vittorio D. Macchioro, *From Orpheus to Paul* (London 1930).

2. (p. 60) See John Pollard, writing on the worship of Helen and Menelaus in *Helen of Troy* (London 1965): 'What remains more doubtful is whether the deity or deities worshipped at Therapne in Mycenaean times, and later, perhaps under the influence of Homer or local poets, identified with the famous hero and heroine, had originally any connection with Helen and her partner at all' (VII, 'Goddess or Heroine', 101).

3. (p. 60) J. D. Unwin, *Sex and Culture* (London 1934), *passim*, esp. paras. 7, 58, 91, 152, 168, and pp. 358–9.

4. (p. 61) This has been disputed: see Aidan Reynolds and William Charlton, *Arthur Machen etc.* (London 1963), 117–18. Whether or not the legend is to be related to the fictional St. George of Machen's 'The Bowmen' (and who knows what may be the true origin of 'fiction'?), some people certainly *thought* that they had seen them. The tendency to believe in and report on such phenomena is too widespread for a facile dismissal: see, e.g., Tacitus, *Histories* v, 13, on the Jewish War. Note too the *imaginative* cogency of 'the great Twin Brethren', Castor and Pollux, in Macaulay's *The Battle of the Lake Regillus*. Macaulay was following Dionysius of Halicarnassus; he has some relevant remarks in his introduction, referring, sceptically, to the supposed appearance of St. James before the army of Cortez in Mexico (*The Lays of Ancient Rome etc.*, Everyman ed., 1963 reprint, 437). We may remember the traditional invocation of St. George by Shakespeare's warriors throughout the History plays; also, and more directly relevant, the use of 'angels' in *Cymbeline* v, iii, 85.

Jackson Knight has an interesting comment on the nature of such experiences 'in times of great stress' in *Vergil: Epic and Anthropology*, ed. John D. Christie (London 1967), 104. For a general discussion of spiritualistic assistance at moments of crisis in both life and literature, see G. Wilson Knight, 'Masefield and Spiritualism' in *Mansions of the Spirit*, ed. George A. Panichas (New York 1967), 268–70. The essay will be reprinted in a forthcoming volume, *Neglected Powers*.

5. (p. 61) For a well-documented discussion of these oracles see now Raymond J. Clark, 'Trophonius: the Manner of his Revelation', *Transactions of the American Philological Association* 99 (1968), 63–75.

6. (p. 61) 'The Drinking Song', reputedly by Callistratus; the text and a discussion are to be found in Sir Maurice Bowra, *Greek Lyric Poetry* (2nd ed. Oxford 1961), 391–6.

7. (p. 63) A. de Buck, *The Egyptian Coffin Texts* (Chicago 1954) v, 209–10; part of Spell 405. The translation by R. T. Rundle Clark was sent to Jackson Knight in 1959.

8. (p. 63) E. B. Tylor, *Primitive Culture* (London 1871 etc.) II, chap. XIII.

9. (p. 64) See the accounts of Parmenides and Empedocles given by Kathleen Freeman, *The Pre-Socratic Philosophers* (Oxford 1946), 140 ff., 172 ff.

NOTES TO CHAPTER 6

1. (p. 66) E. R. Dodds, 'Telepathy and Clairvoyance in Classical Antiquity' in *Greek Poetry and Life, Essays presented to Gilbert Murray* (Oxford 1936), 367.

2. (p. 66) Rohde, *Psyche* (above, IV, note 11), 294–7.

3. (p. 67) The Oracle's mysterious powers have often been discussed. See especially H. W. Parke and D. E. W. Wormell, *The Delphic Oracle* (Oxford 1956) I, 37 ff., where we are referred also (note 91) to a number of other authorities. Of the Delphic prophetess Dodds (above, note 1), 376, writes: 'That the ἐνθουσιασμός of the Pythia and similar personages was at bottom the same psychological condition (when we have allowed for the difference of the organising belief-pattern) as the modern 'mediumistic trance', seems to me reasonably certain: both states are auto-suggestively induced, though not completely dependent on the subject's volition; both are characterised by a temporary but profound disturbance of the sense of identity, together with strong mental excitement and a claim to supernormal knowledge; and both may be followed by amnesia.' For the *absence* of mental excitement in modern trance-mediumship see p. 71 above.

In *The Either-Or of Spiritualism* (London 1928) Mrs. St. Clair Stobart gives an extended attention to Delphi, citing as her main authority A. Bouché-Leclercq, *Histoire de la divination dans l'antiquité* (4 vols., Paris 1879–83).

4. (p. 67) Plutarch says that 'enthusiasm' was usually marked by a change of voice and body (*Quaestiones Conviviales* 623B). Possibly the Pythia spoke in a deep voice when controlled by Apollo. Similar vocal changes are known today. As for the 'change' of 'body', this corresponds to the striking facial changes seen today in what are known as 'transfigura-

tion mediums'; that is, mediums who take on facially the appearance of the communicating personality.

5. (p. 67) The danger of too suddenly awaking a medium *out of* trance is well known, and there may have been a similar danger in forcing a medium *into* trance. Either way a tampering with the same delicate and mysterious mechanism of *transition* (as the word 'trance' denotes) is involved.

6. (p. 72) 'A sibyl of Phrygia, called by some Sarbis (*or* Sarysis) and by some Cassandra, and by others Taraxandra' (Suidas, under 'Sibyl').

7. (p. 73) For discussions of the various exemplars of astral travel, or projection, named below (Aristeas, Abaris, Hermotimus, Epimenides), see Rohde (above, IV, note 11), 300 f.; and, especially, E. R. Dodds, *The Greeks and the Irrational* (Berkeley 1951), 140 ff. J. D. P. Bolton in *Aristeas of Proconnesus* (Oxford 1962) notes many similarities between shamanism and Herodotus' account of Aristeas, but he himself favours a more normal explanation of the events recorded. His book contains an extended list of comparable examples.

Important insights into the nature of projected phantasms are given by Edward Carpenter in *The Drama of Love and Death* (London 1912), 91–2, 128, 148, 164, 182, 265. Carpenter refers us to the standard accounts in *Phantasms of the Living* by E. Gurney, F. W. H. Myers and F. Podmore (London 1886) and *Human Personality and its Survival of Bodily Death* by F. W. H. Myers (London 1903). See also above, II, note 6, on R. Crookall.

For accounts of the projection of the phantasms of Byron and John Cowper Powys during their lives, see G. Wilson Knight, *Byron and Shakespeare* (London 1966), 312–3, 316, and *The Saturnian Quest* (London 1964), 128–9.

NOTES TO CHAPTER 7

1. (p. 74) Cf. Plato, *Phaedo* 64A: 'All those who pursue philosophy aright study nothing but dying and being dead.'

2. (p. 75) Cf. above, II, note 2, on Osiris. In 'The After-Life . . .' (above, IV, note 6), 220, Jackson Knight attributed the statement that 'generally a death-cult and a fertility cult belong together in a single complex' to

'the late and immensely learned Charles Autran'. In his review of Autran's *Homère et les origines sacerdotales de l'épopée grecque* (3 vols., Paris 1938–44) and *L'épopée indoue, étude de l'arrière-fonds ethnographique et religieux* (Paris 1946), he wrote, following Autran: 'At the other end of the span of time, and in, or near, the beginning, the respect for liquid as the source of life, and its pervasive symbolisation in ideogram and cult, help in showing how the *tendance* of the great dead and fertility ritual belong together.' (*The Journal of Hellenic Studies* 72 (1952), 128).

The specific references to Autran were made to indicate that on this central matter of life-death identification (so crucial to our understanding of tragic ritual), we have the support of his abnormally wide range of ethnological learning.

3. (p. 75) *Archiv für Religionswissenschaft* 18 (1915), 116–26.

4. (p. 76) See Sophocles, *Oedipus Tyrannus* 211, 1105; Euripides, *Bacchae*, *passim*.

5. (p. 77) Cf. Heraclitus, 'Hades and Dionysus . . . are the same', Fragment 15, Diels-Kranz. This with other such references to Dionysus as lord of souls is discussed by Rohde in *Psyche* (above, IV, note II), 168, 271, ix. II; cf. also John Pollard, *Seers, Shrines and Sirens* (London 1965), 86, 89. For Osiris as god both of fertility and of Hades see above, II, note 2.

Ibsen was aware of the identification, regarding Dionysus as the god of spirit-communion and spiritualistic practices in *Emperor and Galilean* (*The Emperor Julian* I, i; ed. William Archer, v, 239). Nietzsche's reading of Dionysus as the god of tragic mysticism is a central contribution (*The Birth of Tragedy, passim*).

6. (p. 77) For the religious cults of the Getae, see Rohde (above, IV, note II), 263–5.

7. (p. 78) The thesis was powerfully argued by Sir William Ridgeway in *The Origin of Tragedy* (Cambridge 1910) and *Dramas and Dramatic Dances* (Cambridge 1915).

NOTES TO CHAPTER 8

1. (p. 80) Thales' belief in the individual soul has been disputed on the grounds that soul, *psyche*, for Thales refers simply to hylozoistic matter:

but Diogenes Laertius (I, 24) states that at least Choerilus of Iasus and others understood Thales as meaning that soul was immortal. See G. S. Kirk and J. E. Raven, *The Presocratic Philosophers* (Cambridge 1960), 93–7.

2. (p. 80) *Essays: Classical* (London 1883 etc.), 71, citing Athenagoras, *Legatio pro Christianis*, 23.

3. (p. 81) See Kathleen Freeman, *The Pre-Socratic Philosophers* (Oxford 1946), 28.

4. (p. 81) According to Diogenes Laertius (VIII, 77) he stated: 'For I have once already been a boy and a girl, a bush and a bird, and a dumb fish of the sea.' See further, p. 133 above.

5. (p. 82) Freeman (above, note 3), 183, 187.

NOTES TO CHAPTER 9

1. (p. 87) Ghosts and tombs are among the evidences adduced by Sir William Ridgeway for his reference of tragedy to a death-cult. See above, VII, note 7.

2. (p. 88) Euripides was not mentioned in my brother's original text, and the addition is mine. The *Alcestis* was, I think, the first Greek drama which he read at Dulwich, and I have found on a letter a brief comment, which I think is his, unequivocally asserting its importance.

For *The Bacchae* see E. R. Dodds, *The Bacchae* (2nd ed. Oxford 1960), Introduction. (G.W.K.)

3. (p. 89) I may perhaps point here to my own interpretation of Dionysus' conflict with the chorus of Frogs while crossing the Styx. In *The Golden Ladyrinth* (London 1962), 15–16, I wrote: 'These frogs are creatures of cold, reptilian life, recalling Aeschylus' snaky-haired Furies, and their similarly repetitive and subhuman noises. So Dionysus is really being shown as having to surmount the lower elements of the "Dionysian" in order to enter the realms of Death; and when he gets there, he at once finds another *contrasted* chorus of the initiates in Elysium hymning 'Iacchus', a deity sometimes associated with Dionysus as mystery god. The journey accordingly appears to represent Dionysus' self-surmounting from nature-deity to god of tragedy and Elysian intimations.'

In discussion of *The Birds* I was concerned (16–17) to suggest an analogy between Aristophanes' Birds and the Spirit Beings of modern Spiritualism, Zeus corresponding to the God of orthodox Christianity.

(G.W.K.)

NOTES TO CHAPTER 10

1. (p. 91) The account of survival developed towards the end of the *Phaedo* appears peculiarly interesting in its reading of the new life as located not so much in another work as in a *new dimension of this one*, like a butterfly from a chrysalis. With this description we may profitably compare a report by James McLintock of a conversation between the spirit of Sir Arthur Conan Doyle and Mr. Harry Price, published in *Psychic News*, 12 September 1959. Doyle said:

> I did not recognise the difficulty there would be in getting through this wall or density that stands between us. I am within the solar system but outside your sympathetic system—if I can geographically explain myself.
>
> I would like you to know my location—that I am in a nebulous belt lying outside the earth's surface and having life and being because it has the same structure and matter as the earth itself. I am in no doubt as to my geographical position.

This passage, copied out by Jackson Knight, was found among his papers.

2. (p. 94) Our account of the *Axiochus* is composed of extracts from W. F· Jackson Knight, 'Axiochus', *Pegasus* (Univ. of Exeter) 1, June 1964.

3. (p. 94) Clearchus, quoted by Proclus, *in Rempublicam* II, 122, 22 ff· (ed. Kroll): 'He struck the boy with the wand [earlier regarded as magical], drew out his soul, and, so to speak, guided it from the body with the wand, afterwards showing that the body was all the time lying motionless and undamaged, and that it remained insensible to the blows like a corpse. The soul had meanwhile departed from the body: after having been led back to the body with the help of the wand, after entering, it told all [what it had seen]. This experiment convinced all the other spectators as well as Aristotle that the soul could separate itself from the body.' (Trans. by H. Lewy; see below.)

Clearchus of Soli was a follower of Aristotle, and this fragment is preserved from his dialogue entitled 'On Sleep'. Interesting discussions on the fragment will be found in J. Croissant, *Aristote et les Mystères* (Paris 1932) and H. Lewy, 'Aristotle and the Jewish Sage according to Clearchus of Soli', *Harvard Theological Review* 31 (1938), 205–35.

4. (p. 95) The question of darkness in relation to both the materialisation of spirit-forms and to photography is acutely analysed by Carpenter (above, VI, note 7). More generally, we might compare the use of several curtains 'ensuring complete darkness' in the Hebrew Tabernacle; see Arthur S. Peake, *A Commentary on the Bible* (London 1919), note on Exodus XXVI, 'The Dwelling', 190.

5. (p. 96) Published as 'Creation', an article in *Comment*, Journal of The Marylebone Spiritualist Association, now The Spiritualist Association of Great Britain; Vol. II, No. 2 (1958), 1–15. The general argument corresponds to that of Carpenter (above, VI, note 7). See also 'The Queer World of Quanta', *T.L.S.*, 12 December 1968.

NOTES TO CHAPTER 11

1. (p. 97) Two examples were given by Jackson Knight in *Cumaean Gates* (*Vergil: Epic and Anthropology*, above, IV, note 3, 274): Bruno Traven, *The Death Ship* (London 1934) and Graham Sutton, *The Damnation of Mr. Zinkler* (London 1935). To these we might add: A. Conan Doyle, *The Maracot Deep etc.* (London 1929) and John Cowper Powys, *Morwyn* (London 1937). See also our next note.

2. (p. 97) Two noteworthy modern examples are: James Bramwell, *Going West* (London 1935) and John Cowper Powys, *Atlantis* (London 1954). For Atlantis, see also Bramwell's *Lost Atlantis* (London 1937; reviewed by Jackson Knight in *The Criterion* 17, 1938, 381–2); and Dennis Wheatley, *They Found Atlantis* (London 1936). Powys' and Wheatley's narratives are also interesting in the *genre* of underworld descents (see preceding note); as are also parts of Michael Ayrton's *The Maze Maker* (London 1967). Powys' and Ayrton's re-creations of ancient mythology make a fascinating comparison: the two books should be read together.

3. (p. 98) A *Descent of Orpheus* will be found in O. Kern, *Orphicorum Fragmenta* (Berlin 1922), Fragments 293–6. Cf. the text of a recently

discovered Orphic poem, possibly a Descent, on a Bologna papyrus, first published and discussed by R. Merkelbach (with a foreword by A. Vogliano) in 'Eine orphische Unterweltsbeschreibung auf Papyrus', *Museum Helveticum* 8 (1951), 1–11. This text has been well discussed by R. Turcan, 'La catabase orphique du papyrus de Bologne', *Revue de l'Histoire des Religions* 150 (1956), 136–172. For the literary treatment of Orpheus' descent see M. Owen Lee, 'Orpheus and Eurydice', *Classica et Mediaevalia* 26 (1967), 402–12.

4. (p. 99) Cf. R. Crookall, *The Study and Practice of Astral Projection* (London 1961), 13 and elsewhere. In my own experience a spirit-communicator once, while taking control of a medium, told me that it felt like descending through a dark tunnel to a world of fog. A similar image was used by Wilfred Owen in 'Strange Meeting'.   (G.W.K.)

5. (p. 99) The Petelia and Eleuthernae tablets, translated and discussed in Jane Harrison's *Prolegomena to the Study of Greek Religion* (Cambridge 1903), 573–5, 660–2.

6. (p. 100) See H. Frankfort, *Kingship and the Gods* (Chicago 1948), 62.

7. (p. 101) See E. B. Tylor, *Primitive Culture* (London 1871 etc.) II, 34.

8. (p. 101) For an extended treatment of mazes in general, and for the substance, with references, of the following pages here, see W. F. Jackson Knight, *Cumaean Gates*, 1936; re-issued, revised, in *Vergil: Epic and Anthropology*, ed. John D. Christie (London 1967).

9. (p. 102) We have for clarity slightly expanded the author's text. Here, as in *Cumaean Gates* (revised ed., see preceding note, 143), Jackson Knight had appeared to be identifying the Sibyl's oracular cave with the near-by cave entrance to the underworld beside Lake Avernus through which the Sibyl guides Aeneas. Whether this is an intentional identification is not clear. While composing *Cumaean Gates*, he wrote to me (G.W.K.) on 22 April 1935 that the Sixth *Aeneid* was 'in a sense all cave'. Imaginatively, and for the purposes of his thesis in *Cumaean Gates*, there is little distinction: it is, in a sense, all one 'cave', dominated by the Sibyl.

10. (p. 104) For the labyrinths at Hawara and Cnossos, cf. Jackson Knight (above, note 8), 192.

11. (p. 104) For an interesting link between the children's game of Hopscotch and the labyrinth, see Roger Caillois, *Man, Play and Games*, trans. Meyer Barash (London 1962), 59 and 82.

12. (p. 105) See 'Acheron Shrine Discovered: Oracle of the Dead in Labyrinth' in *The Times*, 17 February 1959, p. 8, col. 4.

NOTE TO CHAPTER 12

1. (p. 111) Our last two paragraphs are taken from an essay by Jackson Knight entitled 'Roman Ideas about Death', a lecture addressed to the Exeter Branch of the Classical Association in October 1951 (see p. 8 above). This essay, which contains a detailed examination of the difficult words *manes, lares and genii*, we hope to publish in a subsequent volume. See also R. B. Onians, *The Origins of European Thought* (Cambridge 1951), esp. II, 2, '*Genius, Numen*, etc.'

A valuable discussion of the Temple of Vesta as 'the abode of the ancestral spirit or spirits of Rome' has recently been published by K. R. Prowse in 'The Vestal Circle', *Greece and Rome* 14 (1967), 174–87.

NOTES TO CHAPTER 13

1. (p. 115) Chrysippus in Suidas under τιμωροῦντος: Cicero, *De Divinatione* I, 57; Valerius Maximus, I, vii, *De Somniis Externorum* 10. The story was rehandled by Chaucer in the course of 'The Nun's Priest's Tale' in *The Canterbury Tales*.

2. (p. 117) For a recent account of such phenomena, see John Pollard, *Wolves and Werewolves* (London 1964).

NOTES TO CHAPTER 14

1. (p. 120) See C. J. De Vogel, *Greek Philosophy* (Leiden 1959) III, 95–6, para. 957, citing Epiphanius, Arius Didymus, and Diogenes Laertius.

2. (p. 120) For a discussion of 'The Dream of Scipio' with a useful list of the relevant literature, see De Vogel (above, note 1) III, 98–9, para. 959.

3. (p. 122) On Lucretius and Epicurus, see now George A. Panichas, *Epicurus* (New York 1967).

4. (p. 123) Franz Cumont, *After Life in Roman Paganism* (New York 1922), 22, 97.

5. (p. 123) On the evidence of paranormal powers in Nigidius, see Dodds, 'Telepathy . . . ' (above, VI, note 1), 384.

6. (p. 123) Cf. R. M. Ogilvie's discussion in his *Commentary on Livy, Books 1–5* (Oxford 1965), 89–90. See K. R. Prowse, 'Numa and the Pythagoreans: a Curious Incident', *Greece and Rome* II (1964), 36–42.

NOTES TO CHAPTER 15

1. (p. 126) T. J. Haarhoff, *Vergil the Universal* (Oxford 1949).

2. (p. 127) Cf. W. F. Jackson Knight, *Roman Vergil* (London 1944; revised and enlarged, Penguin Books 1966), ch. III.

3. (p. 128) For an extensive treatment of the esoteric content of the Sixth *Aeneid*, see W. F. Jackson Knight, *Cumaean Gates* (above, XI, note 8).

4. (p. 129) See W. F. Jackson Knight, *Roman Vergil* (above, note 2), 248.

5. (p. 133) The interpretation in our text corresponds in general with that advanced independently by R. D. Williams in 'The Sixth Book of the *Aeneid*', *Greece and Rome* II (1964), 57–8. Williams argues that Vergil's final paradise is not Elysium but an 'ultimate paradise' beyond. Vergil is scarcely explicit: Jackson Knight's 'lives, apparently, in bliss for ever' indicates a certain hesitation; but this seems to be the meaning. The main distinction depends on our reading the passage 'and we few . . . elemental fire' (*et pauci . . . simplicis ignem*, 744–7) as a rather awkward parenthesis, with the following 'all these souls' (*has omnis*, 748) harking back to the others. One has to imagine a gesture.

6. (p. 135) The imaginative authority of the vision already presented need not be in any important sense negated by such a subsequent, off-hand, repudiation by the poet, if indeed there is one, as is here suggested.

(G.W.K.)

NOTE TO CHAPTER 16

1. (p. 141) An excellent survey of Seneca's views, with many references, is given in Franz Cumont, *Lux Perpetua* (Paris 1949), 164–70.

NOTES TO CHAPTER 17

1. (p. 145) These events are more fully described by Jackson Knight in his extended account of Apollonius in three issues of *Psychic News* (Nos. 1564–6; 26 May, 2 and 9 June 1962).

For his descriptions of Apollonius' psychic powers Philostratus claims to have relied mainly on a manuscript by Damis, a friend of Apollonius. There has been much controversy regarding the biography from the time of its first appearance until now. It has been variously regarded both as a source and as a derivative of the Gospels. Such confusions appear to have arisen from a reluctance to acknowledge the generality of the paranormal.

2. (p. 145) Mr. Hugh Stubbs suggests that the belief in demonic possession would perhaps spread the more naturally among people whose terrain was occupied by a foreign and idolatrous army.

3. (p. 147) A similar problem arises with the Apocryphal Gospels. The New Testament as we know it is a selection from a range of material, some of it fantastic. See *The Apocryphal New Testament*, trans. M. R. James (revised, Oxford 1953).

4. (p. 147) Philostratus' historical accuracy has been defended by F. Grosso in *Acme* (Milan) 7 (1954), 331–532.

NOTES TO CHAPTER 18

1. (p. 149) The Authorised Version reads: 'Then said Saul unto his servants, "Seek me a woman that hath a familiar spirit, that I may go to her and

enquire of her." And his servants said to him, "Behold, there is a woman that hath a familiar spirit at Endor." Saul disguised himself and put on other raiment, and he went, and two men with him, and they came to the woman by night: and he said, "I pray thee, divine unto me by the familiar spirit, and bring me him up, whom I shall name unto thee." '

James Moffatt's *A New Translation of the Bible* (London 1925 etc.) variously uses the terms 'witch', 'wizard' and 'medium', Saul saying: 'Inquire for me as a medium . . .'

The dangers of any discussion of this incident without a knowledge of psychic science, as with the commentators who change 'And when the woman saw Samuel' to 'And when the woman saw Saul', are emphasised by the Rev. G. Maurice Elliott in 'Was the Woman of Endor a Witch?', *The Bible as Psychic History* (London 1959), 117 ff.

In *Man and his Destiny in the Great Religions* (Manchester 1962) S. G. F. Brandon offers a penetrating treatment of Hebraic religion, wherein the rivalry of Jahweh worship and ancient spiritualism is admirably discussed and defined.

2. (p. 150) The psychic and spiritualistic elements of the Old and New Testaments are powerfully handled throughout that classic of Spiritualism, the Rev. Charles L. Tweedale's *Man's Survival after Death; or, The Other Side of Life in the light of Scripture, Human Experience, and Modern Research* (originally London 1909, but valuably amplified in subsequent editions, which contain important new material).

See also the Rev. G. Maurice Elliott, *The Psychic Life of Jesus* (London 1938) and *The Bible as Psychic History* (London 1959).

3. (p. 151) Arthur Findlay, *The Psychic Stream* (London 1939), 699–701, following F. C. Conybeare, *Myth, Magic and Morals* (London 1909), 232–4. Dr. Conybeare's reference to mediumship has support in Arthur S. Peake's note on our passage in *A Commentary on the Bible* (London 1928), 842: 'As Dibellius points out, it is a widespread belief that the veil has magical power. Its function is therefore to ward off dangers. The danger is specially present when the woman prays or prophesies.' Peake here refers to Tertullian, *De Virginibus·Velandis*, 7, and continues: 'Apparently in the ecstatic condition, pressing into the spiritual realm, she is more exposed to the advances of the angels than in her normal condition. Hence she needs a means of protection.'

4. (p. 151) Belief in bodily resurrection is countered by the body's known dissolution at death. Orthodox belief has begun to face the difficulty. In *Doctrine in the Church of England: The Report of the Commission on Christian Doctrine appointed by the Archbishops of Canterbury and York in 1922* (London, S.P.C.K. 1938) it is convincingly argued that the doctrine of bodily resurrection covers the important truths that the new

life is to be no less rich than this that we know and that mutual recognition will be possible. The new body will bear the same relation to the personality concerned as did the old. However, if the two bodies are different, the term 'resurrection' is inexact and misleading. All difficulties are met by the spiritualistic teaching on the 'etheric' or 'astral' body, existing within, or around, the physical body of which it is a simulacrum, to be released at death.

5. (p. 152) The *shophar*, a ram's-horn trumpet, was used to announce 'the death of a notable' (*The Interpreter's Dictionary of the Bible*, ed. George A. Buttrick, New York 1962, III, 473). It 'was sounded at funerals' and also at intervals, as a kind of Last Post, as night was falling on Fridays until the lighting of the Sabbath candles (*The Jewish Encyclopaedia*, ed. Isidore Singer etc., New York and London 1905, XI, 304). The transition from darkness to sacred light bears relevance to our argument.

6. (p. 152) *Doctrine in the Church of England etc.* (above, note 4) admits that the traditional idea of waiting for a single Day of General Resurrection 'presents great difficulties', but believes that, like the Resurrection of the Body, it at least functions as a safeguard of certain valuable truths. It is perhaps time that we should try to formulate the truths concerned without such disturbing inaccuracies.

7. (p. 152) Elliott (above, note 1), 96–7, quoting Sir Arthur Conan Doyle's report of séance phenomena exactly recalling the flames and wind of Pentecost.

8. (p. 153) E. J. Dingwall, *Ghosts and Spirits in the Ancient World* (London 1930), 37, compares the wind in *Gilgamesh* to the many reports of cold breezes accompanying psychic phenomena in our time.

9. (p. 153) Cf. John Pollard, *Wolves and Werewolves* (London 1964), 139.

10. (p. 153) There are other resemblances. As Christ appeared to the disciples after his death and resurrection (Matthew XXVIII, 18–20), so Apollonius appeared after death in a sleep-vision to an apostle who doubted the immortality of the soul, including that of Apollonius (Philostratus, *Vita Apollonii* VIII, 31). As Christ healed the sick and raised Jairus' daughter from death (Mark V, 22 ff.; Luke VIII, 41 ff.), so Apollonius cured the sick and raised a dead girl (*Vita Apollonii* IV, 1; VI, 43; IV, 45). As Paul's and Silas' chains fell off in prison (Acts XVI, 26), so, as we have seen (p. 147), Apollonius while in prison removed his legs from the fetters at will.

11. (p. 155) Marjorie Livingston, *The New Nuctemeron: The Twelve Hours of Apollonius of Tyana* (London 1930). Among the papers left by

Jackson Knight are notes on this book with an acknowledgement: 'I have it through the great kindness of Mrs. Margaret Wilson.'

12. (p. 155) 'Beloved, believe not every spirit, but try the spirits, whether they are of God . . . Hereby know ye the Spirit of God: every spirit that confesseth that Jesus Christ is come in the flesh is of God: and every spirit that confesseth not that Jesus Christ is come in the flesh is not of God.' (John, Epistle I, IV, 1–3; cf. also St. Paul, I Corinthians XII, 3).

13. (p. 155) The statement may be allowed to refer both to Vergil's acceptance as an '*anima naturaliter Christiana*' in the Middle Ages and also to certain evidences of Vergilian communication of which Jackson Knight had received reports.

14. (p. 156) 'And Death and Hades were cast into the lake of fire. This is the second death, even the lake of fire.' Sinners are also said to be cast into the lake: 'And if any was not found written in the book of life, he was cast into the lake of fire' (Revelation XX, 14–15). According to Peake's *Commentary on the Bible*, Death and Hades are here regarded as 'two demonic powers'. In his *New Translation of the Bible*, James Moffatt's shifting of these words on the 'second death' to make them apply only to sinners 'since there is no question of a second death except for human beings', appears to be ill-advised. Cf. G. Wilson Knight, *The Christian Renaissance*, (enlarged ed. London 1962), 195 and note.

15. (p. 157) The teaching of *The New Nuctemeron* shows fascinating correspondences to the thought of our greater writers as discussed in my own various literary studies. The doctrine of salvation by personal effort rather than a vicarious sacrifice is that of Byron's *Manfred* and *Cain* (*Byron and Shakespeare*, London 1966, 176–9, 301, 309). The repudiation of eternal damnation echoes Shakespeare's *Macbeth* I, iii, 24:

> Though his bark cannot be lost,
> Yet it shall be tempest-toss'd.

The respect accorded to adventurous evil in 'a great spirit' bears an obvious relation to the dark protagonists of Shakespearian, and other, dramas (*Shakespeare and Religion*, London 1967, 13–21, 34–6). The potentialities of the human mind were similarly honoured in Wordsworth's lines in his 1814 Preface to *The Excursion* (*The Starlit Dome*, London 1964 ed., 1–2) on the 'fear and awe' which he feels in looking into

> the Mind of Man,
> My haunt, and the main region of my song.

The concept 'superman' recalls Nietzsche. Such correspondences, here and elsewhere, between the teaching of discarnate powers and the products of literary genius are extensive, and of the highest importance to our evolving religious wisdom. (G.W.K.)

16. (p. 157) A closely similar 'scientific' approach empowers the comprehensive analyses of Edward Carpenter's *The Drama of Love and Death* (London 1912).

17. (p. 157) *The New Nuctemeron* may be profitably compared with the equally convincing, and often similar, statements transmitted as from F. W. H. Myers in Geraldine Cummins' *The Road to Immortality* (with a foreword by Sir Oliver Lodge; London 1932) and *Beyond Human Personality* (London 1935).

18. (p. 158) For parallels, with variations, in modern Indian thought, see Sri Aurobindo, *The Life Divine* (2 vols., Calcutta 1939–40); and C. B. Purdom, *The God-Man* (London 1964); a study of the life and teaching of Meher Baba.

NOTES TO CHAPTER 19

1. (p. 159) Norman J. Bull, *The Rise of the Church* (London 1967), 191.

2. (p. 160) For a lucid account of the spiritualistic activities of the early Church, written from an anti-ecclesiastical standpoint, see Arthur Findlay, *The Psychic Stream* (London 1939). Findlay uses the passage from Tertullian's *De Anima* quoted in our text: see p. 20 above.

3. (p. 161) Myers has a footnote: 'It is uncertain where Hesiod places the abode of this class of spirits; the MSS read ἐπιχθόνιοι ['on the earth'], Gaisford (with Tzetzes) and Wolff, *De Daemonibus*, ὑποχθόνιοι ['under the earth'].

4. (p. 162) For Thales see p. 80 and note 1, above. For Pythagoras, Myers cites Porphyry, *Vita Pythagorae*, 384.

5. (p. 166) A translation is available under the title: 'Theurgia or *The Egyptian Mysteries* by Iamblichus'; translated from the Greek by Alexander Wilder (London 1881–5 etc.). An excellent edition has now appeared in the Budé series: E. des Places (ed.), *Jamblique: Les Mystères d'Égypte* (Paris 1966).

In *The Either-Or of Spiritualism* (London 1928), Mrs. St. Clair Stobart gives an outline of the book's contents and emphasises the close correspondence, point by point, of the issues raised to the problems of communication experienced by modern Spiritualism.

6. (p. 169) For extended surveys of St. Augustine's thought in these matters, with references, see E. R. Dodds, 'Telepathy . . .' (above, VI, note I), 382–5; also W. Montgomery, 'St. Augustine's Attitude to Psychic Phenomena' in *The Hibbert Journal* 25 (1926–7), 92–102.

NOTES TO CHAPTER 20

1. (p. 173) It might be argued that Empedocles' two great principles, negative and positive, alternate eternally; but his primary *emphasis* on Love may be said to correspond to the intuition stated in our text. See p. 82 above.

2. (p. 174) For text and references see H. W. Parke and D. E. W. Wormell, *The Delphic Oracle* (Oxford 1956) I, 290; II, 194–5. This last Delphic utterance is discussed by F. W. H. Myers in *Essays: Classical* (London 1883 etc.), 100–1. Cf. also Swinburne's poem *The Last Oracle*.

3. (p. 176) A. P. Stanley, *Lectures on the History of the Eastern Church* (London 1861); Everyman Library ed. (1907, reprinted 1924), 187–8.

4. (p. 176) *Acta Sanctorum*, ed. J. Bolland (revised, Paris 1865), March VII, 669A, 34–5.

5. (p. 177) Boethius is more fully treated in Jackson Knight's 'Virgilio, Plotino, Boezio', *Orpheus* 9 (1962), 3–19, (a lecture delivered to the Centro di studi sull'antico Cristianesimo, Università di Catania, Spring 1961).

Indexes

A. INDEX OF NAMES (selected)

B. INDEX OF THEMES (*selected*)